San Francisco
Confidential

San Francisco Confidential

×××××××××××

Tales of Scandal and Excess From the Town That's Seen Everything

RAY MUNGO

A Birch Lane Press Book
Published by Carol Publishing Group

A Birch Lane Press Book
Published by Carol Publishing Group

Birch Lane Press is a registered trademark of Carol Communications, Inc.

Editorial Offices: 600 Madison Avenue, New York, N.Y. 10022
Sales and Distribution Offices: 120 Enterprise Avenue, Secaucus, N.J. 07094
In Canada: Canadian Manda Group, One Atlantic Avenue, Suite 105, Toronto,
    Ontario M6K 3E7
Queries regarding rights and permissions should be addressed to Carol
    Publishing Group, 600 Madison Avenue, New York, N.Y. 10022

Carol Publishing Group books are available at special discounts for bulk
purchases, sales promotion, fund-raising, or educational purposes. Special
editions can be created to specifications. For details, contact: Special Sales
Department, Carol Publishing Group, 120 Enterprise Avenue, Secaucus, N.J.
07094.

Photo of Golden Gate Bridge at night, 1987, pages iv–v, courtesy AP/Wide
World Photos.

Manufactured in the United States of America
10 9 8 7 6 5 4 3 2 1

Library of Congress Cataloging-in-Publication Data

Mungo, Raymond, 1946–
    San Francisco confidential : tales of scandal and excess from the town that's
seen everything / by Ray Mungo.
        p.   cm.
    "A Birch Lane Press book."
    ISBN 1-55972-246-0
    1. Popular culture—California—San Francisco—History. 2. Scandals—
California—San Francisco—History. 3. San Francisco (Calif.)—Social life and
customs.   I. Title.
F869.S35M86   1994   94-12615
979.4'61—dc20   CIP

Dedication

Angus Mackenzie, the founder of the Center for Investigative Reporting in San Francisco, died in March 1994 at the untimely age of forty-three. Right to the end, he lived in a cute, ramshackle wooden house in the Bernal Heights neighborhood of the City, as San Francisco is simply called by those who know her well. (And never "Frisco," of course.) Although he wasn't born there (is anybody?), San Francisco was Angus's home for many years, and the City and man belonged together, joined in passion and madness.

Angus was crazy, you might say, but I mean no disrespect. If the average American were to encounter Angus, he'd say, now there's a crazy guy. Long-ponytailed, bearded, forever wildly gesticulating and delivering fiery denunciations, driving around in his beat-up 1952 truck, Angus was a San Francisco "character." He practically invented the federal Freedom of Information Act, that is, he was one of the first to use it to pry information from the public records, and he was a relentless crusader for the civil rights guaranteed by the Constitution. It was Angus who revealed that the feds had infiltrated and sabotaged the student and "alternative" underground newspapers of the 1960s, suppressing freedom of speech and possibly even murdering a few of the more outspoken journalists.

Dedication

Murder is nothing new in San Francisco. People actually get away with it. Look at Dan White, with his laughable sentence of seven years, eight months (of which he served only half) for murdering the sitting mayor, George Moscone (literally sitting at his desk), and openly gay supervisor, Harvey Milk. It was Angus who first told me that Dan White himself was gay, ashamed of it and hiding in the closet. Later, I got the story confirmed by a second source, a longtime *Chronicle* beat reporter. But Angus knew everybody's secrets. For example, how the guy who founded Victoria's Secret, the ladies' lingerie chain, got so desperate that he jumped off the Golden Gate Bridge. It's in this book.

San Francisco can't keep a secret very well. The City is a shameless gossip. A book like this is just a compilation of gossipry past and present. For some reason, San Francisco seems to outdo every other place for sheer drama, surprising twists of fate, oddities, social eccentricities, "characters." Oh, New York and L.A. and other great huge cities are much larger and have more gross weight of crime and misdemeanor, but San Francisco pulls off its scandals with style, with brioche.

For starters, the City is geographically spectacular, and that's something you just can't replicate elsewhere. Nobody has ever seen San Francisco for the first time without losing a breath. The ridiculously steep hills leading down to the impossibly blue Bay, the fog, the nearby mountains and beaches: the whole setting is precipitous. Dangerously beautiful. Too rich, too gorgeous to last. Live fast, die young, make a beautiful corpse.

In this setting of dramatic beauty, for some reason the human pulse beats faster, and social drama, too, is heightened. People fall in love in San Francisco. Of course Tony Bennett left his heart there. People come to San Francisco to abandon their old life, shed previous identities and emerge anew, a different person, in an environment that encourages differentness. Every kind of radical social movement you can think of thrives in San Francisco—many were born there. The City gives people a kind of license to create, to foment, to dance and clash and sparkle.

The price of all this colorful excitement is commensurately steep. The City seems fatally attracted to every kind of catastrophe. The Great Earthquake of 1906 was just a prelude to the greater one to come. The suicide rate is much higher than the mean in United States cities, but other cities don't have that gorgeous Golden Gate Bridge beckoning the despondent to its orange arms, and in order to protect the view the City has resisted all efforts to construct safety guardrails.

Naturally the AIDS epidemic would find its greatest population of victims in San Francisco. Even now, people with AIDS often move to San Francisco from other places to get the tender advantage of superior care and caring in their final days. Of course, the high infection rate is also a consequence of having the nation's highest concentration of gay men per capita. But every population-at-risk knows the streets of San Francisco. The homeless are numerous, aggressively aware of their rights, and politically significant in the City. The intravenous drug users are ubiquitous in the Haight, the Tenderloin, and the fine marble homes of Pacific Heights. The prostitutes have rightly considered San Francisco home territory since 1850, and what other city has an annual Hookers' Ball that is a "must" event for high society? The impoverished Asian refugee has been a mainstay San Francisco character from Day One, when boatloads of indentured Chinese workers were dumped off there to build the railroads for the bigot barons.

Any kind of fire, drought, economic depression, gruesome homicide, traffic mishap, death by sex torture, or act of random kindness is commonplace in the City That Knows How, or knew how when that quaint slogan was coined ages ago.

Financial mayhem is virtually the foundation of the City's fiscal superstructure. The City was born in the mad pursuit of gold, remember, when thousands of single men cascaded into the area to stake claims in the rich Sierra Nevada. Since then, San Francisco has always been expensive. The cost of living is right up there with Honolulu, New York, and Tokyo. Rents are especially high, and real estate is astronomical; drinks in a sawdust-floor saloon are still dirt cheap, however. I haven't seen any statistics to prove it, but common sense will tell you there are more bars per person in San Francisco than anywhere else in the country except New Orleans, which is kind of an alcoholic Disneyland. Neighborhoods still have tiny, smoke-filled taverns where the regulars all know each other and the occasional stranger is welcomed warmly—unless, of course, he's the wrong color or not Irish or some other sin. San Francisco's deeply Catholic and guilt-driven because of it. Saint Francis, you know. A Sissi.

Some of the best conversation in the world can be found in those

Dedication

saloons. The gift of gab is never in short supply in San Francisco. Maybe that's why Angus's secrets and everybody's secrets about the place not only come out in the open but get exaggerated, tossed around, and replayed in the media to cartoony excess. Nothing can remain hidden for long.

Angus's conclusion, which would certainly be debated by the politicians and corrupt officials, was that the City is now out of control, as it was long ago. All efforts to civilize San Francisco have failed. The authorities can't stem the tide of illegal immigrants, halt the drug trade, get the prostitutes off the streets, tax the black market economy, or otherwise get a real grip on things. You could compare San Francisco to Hong Kong. Anything goes.

Angus's other conclusion was that it didn't matter a good goddamn whether the authorities could control San Francisco as long as the people had food on their tables and solid walls against the biting cold wind off the fog-shrouded Bay, and hunkered down in their neighborhoods and would not be moved. And as long as they didn't develop an inoperable brain tumor that would kill a man of forty-three, as it did Angus.

So this work is dedicated to him and the City that gave him a home.

Contents

Contents

Contents

Everyone who is reported missing is sooner or later said to have been seen in San Francisco

—OSCAR WILDE

San Francisco Confidential

Introduction:
Walking
on Air

There is a certain quality of make-believe in San Francisco's very soul, as if the place is unreal. Oh, it's real enough if you're shivering in the fog, bent under the cruel winds of summer whipping up Mission Street, or down and out in the Tenderloin. But the City obscures the line between fantasy and actuality, and the most fantastical things can happen here.

A man becomes a woman, then a nun, then an angel to AIDS patients. A politician smokes a joint on the Sausalito ferry deck. The Episcopal bishop claims he believes in UFOs. A student at Berkeley sheds his clothing in a passionate crusade for the right to be naked in public—and it's not that warm in Berkeley. Castro Street teems with creatures of unimaginable appearance, and not just on Halloween. Brownie Mary passes out pot pastries to suffering victims in hospital beds. And still, always, Herb Caen checks in with a fresh column in the morning paper.

William Randolph Hearst III, relation to Patty, publishes the *Examiner* in the afternoon, but everybody reads the *Chronicle* in the morning instead, except when Caen is on vacation and its circulation drops 30 percent in the City. The papers combine on Sunday in a joint edition, and both carry the same classified ad section every day. You have only one place to sell that bicycle or real estate.

She's a small town, San Francisco, a city proper with fewer than a million residents, yet blessed with universal name recognition.

She's an "old whore of a town who's seen everything," as the immortal Herb Caen observed.

She's the crown princess of sex, sleaze, and scandal in the United States, rivaled only by New Orleans for hedonistic excess. Yet she's suave, genteel, and stylish.

She's San Francisco, "Baghdad by the Bay," everyone's favorite city. A bad, bad girl with a Golden Gate and a heart of gold, Boys' Town for some, Babylon for others, a temptress, a stud, a state of mind.

From the Gold Rush of 1849 through the homeless riots of 1993, San Francisco has been the nation's bellwether of chaos, opportunity, controversy, extravagance. The last great city in America to outlaw prostitution (in 1914), San Francisco is seriously considering making it legal again. The most liberal and compassionate of cities now strikes back against a huge, overwhelming population of street people. Here, the assassin of the mayor and a supervisor gets off with a few short years in jail on a "Twinkie" defense, junk food leading to double homicide. Here, a deadly earthquake intersects a cross-Bay World Series.

Everything and anything is possible under the arches of the seductive Golden Gate. Here, Carol Doda reinvented topless dancing, the Beatniks rekindled American literature, Bill Graham birthed the rock and roll concert, and the Beatles packed Candlestick Park in their last public appearance ever.

It's fashionable in the late part of this century to say that San Francisco has gone downhill, that it's not the elegant place it once was, that it's gone to the dogs, like so many other American cities. Certainly, the City has problems. Crime and squalor are everywhere, sin and scandal rampant. But since when has it ever been otherwise in this place?

San Francisco was founded in a condition of criminal anarchy. Chinatown was the center of an open female slave trade. The saloons and stills were murderous places during the heady years of the Gold Rush. Absolute lawlessness reigned until the underworld known as the Barbary Coast was wiped out by the great fire following the 1906 earthquake. The tradition of prostitution, public drunkenness, and debauchery continues, however, to the present day.

Led by the bigot Leland Stanford, who later was governor of California, the Big Four railroad barons imported thousands of Chinese laborers to build the Central Pacific and effectively created the ramshackle San Francisco Chinatown, which attracted hoodlums and the slave and drug trades. These early beginnings assured San Francisco's reputation as the most sexually permissive place in the United States.

The Great Earthquake and Fire of 1906 was widely viewed as parallel to the destruction of Sodom and Gomorrah, definitely God's punishment on San Francisco for its immorality. Sure enough, the 1989 earthquake produced similar declarations from extremists of the religious right wing, this time because of the City's homosexual population and soaring AIDS rate.

As San Francisco grew and prospered, bridges were constructed to link its thumb-like peninsula, three-quarters surrounded by water, to the mainland. Not long after the magnificent Golden Gate Bridge opened in May 1937, the first of many despondent people jumped off. The dreamy span now owns the regrettable distinction of being the world's favorite place to commit suicide. Somebody jumps every three weeks, on average. The clerks in the souvenir shop can see the bodies drop. A recent one was Roy Raymond, the tortured entrepreneur who founded the Victoria's Secret sexy lingerie chain.

Pulitzer Prize–winning playwright William Saroyan characterized the alcoholic nature of San Francisco in his play *The Time of Your Life*, which opened in 1941 and was set in a Tenderloin bar. All the characters drift in and out of the saloon on a single day. The City is famous for its watering holes, and the older ones have a rich history. If you drop into Lefty O'Doul's in Union Square for an afternoon Bloody Mary, the bartender might tell you why O'Doul, a locally born outfielder who played for the Phillies (1928–35) and in the Pacific Coast League, should be in the Hall of Fame.

Only San Francisco could have given us the Beat Generation, born in the 1950s. Lawrence Ferlinghetti, Jack Kerouac, Allen Ginsberg, City Lights Books, and hundreds of wild characters formed the cutting edge of a real poetry revolution in North Beach, the reverberations of which reached everywhere in the world. Kerouac and his *On the Road* buddy

Neal Casady shared the sexual favors of Neal's wife, Carolyn, as well as sleeping with each other.

A relatively talentless but enormously endowed performer named Carol Doda popularized topless dancing in North Beach in the early 1960s and became as famous a symbol of San Francisco as the bridge itself. For a number of years, San Francisco was the only place in America where it was legal for women to bare their breasts in public. Bottomless dancing followed, of course.

Janis Joplin was Carol's counterpart by the late 1960s, a singer who personified San Francisco in its Summer of Love (1967) and spent most of her time here, drinking epic amounts of Jack Daniels, consuming drugs, and sleeping with legions of admirers. Janis was out of control and died young. The City rocked on. The Grateful Dead is still considered a local band.

The Rolling Stones concert at Altamont, near Oakland, was billed as a California version of Woodstock in 1969, but the crowd went berserk, the Hell's Angels got rough, and death and mayhem resulted. By 1970, San Francisco was considered more dangerous than New York City.

It could be said that psychedelic rock and roll originated in the City with producer Bill Graham and his throbbing Fillmore and Avalon ballrooms. Graham's unbridled pizzazz launched groups like the Dead, Big Brother and the Holding Company, Country Joe and the Fish, and many more. Acid rock was born at Muir Beach, where thousands tripped and rocked en masse.

Naturally, the LSD culture and acid consciousness were more evident in San Francisco than elsewhere. Ken Kesey and his Merry Pranksters caromed around Haight Ashbury in their flamboyantly painted bus. Timothy Leary found acceptance and even respectability after being ousted from the faculty at Harvard. While not legal in San Francisco, "soft" drugs like pot or acid, in small personal quantity, were virtually ignored by the police, and still are. People smoked joints openly on the streets and passed them around to strangers.

The People's Temple, led by the Reverend Jim Jones, came out of San Francisco but wound up in a gruesome mass suicide in the jungles of Guyana. Jim Jones's story is a fascinating study in corruption. At one time he was an important civic figure in town, invited to mayoral receptions and holding sway over high society gatherings. He served

Carol Doda struts her stuff at the Condor Club in San Francisco, 1969.
(*Bettmann*)

on public commissions and could deliver votes. But in 1978, his megalomaniacal passions led him to orchestrate the Kool-Aid cyanide deaths of 912 followers in the steamy crypt named Jonestown, while all of San Francisco cringed.

Ex-supervisor Dan White crawled into City Hall through a bathroom window, armed to the teeth, and shot and killed Mayor George Moscone and gay supervisor Harvey Milk in cold blood, yet he got off with a paltry eight-year sentence after mounting a defense based on his diet of Twinkies and other junk food and his standing as a patriotic, God-fearing, churchgoing former cop. What the jury didn't hear was that the fiercely homophobic Dan White was himself gay and sleeping with a city fireman. His twisted story came to a grim end in yet another suicide by the Bay.

The Mitchell brothers were pioneers of modern pornography in the City, and their name still adorns the marquee of the famous adult movie house on Polk Street where the feature *Behind the Green Door* is playing in its third decade. Jim and Artie Mitchell, although entrepreneurs of sleaze, were known to be good fellows and civic stalwarts until Jim shot and killed Artie and, predictably, got off with a light sentence. Historically, murder seems tolerated in San Francisco more than in most cities.

The AIDS epidemic in San Francisco, especially in the Castro District, is a phenomenon almost too painful to report, but the City became the first American gay mecca and consequently was and is the hardest hit by AIDS. From the flamboyant excesses of the Gay Pride Parade to the heroic writings of Randy Shilts, the City has known license, love, and suffering beyond any other.

The '90s have brought new joys, nightmares, soap operas, and fairy tales. Berserko mobs of in-line skaters, hand in hand, zoom twelve miles across the city every Friday night, terrorizing pedestrians and motorists alike. The Golden Gate Bridge operators have taken to keeping hard liquor on hand as an enticement to make people reconsider jumping. In suburban Petaluma, twelve-year-old Polly Klaas was kidnapped from her own bedroom while horrified classmates, having a pajama party, looked on. The town, the whole Bay Area, searched for the missing girl without success.

Herb Caen keeps cranking out his daily column in the *Chronicle*,

1991. The Mitchell brothers, owners of the O'Farrell Theatre, would later become the Cain and Abel of San Francisco burlesque after the shooting of Artie (left) by his brother Jim (right). (*AP/Wide World Photos*)

easily the most popular feature in a newspaper that's seen better times. A strange bug called phylloxera has been killing off the famous vineyards of Napa, source of the City's proud wine stock. A fifty-three-year-old City cop, Bob Geary, won a narrow victory in a referendum allowing him to use his ventriloquist's dummy, Brendan O'Smarty, on his beat patrol. "See? A wooden personality is not a drawback," cracked Caen.

Outside the search headquarters for Polly Klass, 1993. (*Bettmann*)

Introduction: Walking on Air

A widely circulated, serious proposal to divide the state of California into two independent states originated—where else?—in San Francisco. Locals here still think of Los Angeles as the great demon to the south, and the intensity of hatred (rivalry is too wimpy a word for it) toward the Dodgers when they visit the Giants at Candlestick Park is stunning to an outsider.

The current police chief, Tony Ribera, is known for "going ballistic" and losing his temper in public. The previous one, Richard Hongisto, was fired by Mayor Frank Jordan after he seized and destroyed thousands of copies of a gay and lesbian magazine that criticized him. Hongisto was also accused of sexually harassing women employees. Perhaps Brendan O'Smarty would like the job.

The homeless community has started an organic vegetable garden at the corner of Divisadero and Ellis, but the problem now is keeping other homeless people from possibly stealing the produce right off the vine. Everyone, but everyone, was upset when female impersonator and local celebrity Jim Bailey was bounced from the cast of *Jeffrey*, a gay comedy about AIDS imported from New York. An empty lot in Berkeley has been filled with discarded toilets and christened the New Sense Museum (say it fast). In perhaps a related incident, artist Richard List propped a ladder against the San Francisco Museum of Art and hung toilet seat covers from the building facade until arrested by police. He called it "plop art."

Mayor Jordan decided to blame the City's problems on the homeless, leading to a nefarious program called Operation Matrix, the whole purpose of which seems to be to make poverty a crime. City police now attack the group called Food Not Bombs, which distributes nourishment to the destitute. Pending a court appeal, it's now illegal to push a shopping cart or sleep in the streets of San Francisco.

Meanwhile, ambitious young hotelier Chip Conley took the derelict Phoenix Inn in one of the most rundown parts of town, Larkin at Eddy, and turned it into a famous gathering place for rock and roll musicians and their admirers. John F. Kennedy Jr. stayed there for $125 a night, although you have to fight your way through the homeless beggars and public drunks to get in.

New evidence strongly suggests that the Oakland–San Francisco Bay Bridge may not withstand another major earthquake, of which there is a 67 percent likelihood in the next thirty years in the Bay Area.

If the Bay Bridge should collapse, not only would the cost in human lives be tragic, but the area's economy would be crippled for years.

People with AIDS have opened a "marijuana supermarket" in the 700 block of Castro Street that sells pot for medicinal use. Cancer patients, chemotherapy recipients, and victims of other diseases also benefit from the San Francisco Cannabis Buyers Club, organized in 1971 by Dennis Peron, whose deceased lover had used grass to lessen his pain and nausea. If the police know of this buyers' club, they haven't made any moves against it, despite its being an open secret.

The water in San Francisco Bay is so polluted and overexploited that experts agree the Bay itself is in peril. Some water species are already extinct, others endangered, and the human peril from toxic waste and sewage is frightening. Yet there is no coherent plan to save this body of water from the ravages of overuse.

But poetry is still doing fine in San Francisco, even though the Beats are long gone. A new program puts City poets' timeless lines on display on ATM machines at Wells Fargo Bank branches and on the Muni city bus electronic information signs. "J Street Bus Next—Ah, windblown Golden Gate raga of sex and suicide!"

Will there ever be a new baseball stadium to replace the Arctic outpost called Candlestick Park? The City has been embroiled in this issue for thirty years. Apparently the old New York Giants owner, Horace Stoneham, was always taken to see the Candlestick building site in the mornings. The wind picks up in the afternoon, and by night the cold is numbing, even in July.

The Gallo family and their famous northern California winery have long figured in San Francisco's mythology and economy. The original Gallo brothers, Joe and Mike, staked their venture on bootlegging and extortion money. Joe killed his wife, Susie, and then himself on a bloody, mysterious night in Fresno. His three sons quarreled bitterly over the family assets.

Also quarreling bitterly were opponents and supporters of a system that allowed the director of the San Francisco Zoo to move out of his official house at the zoo into a $24,000-a-year apartment at city expense. His free rent was on top of a salary of $98,000, and after four years in the free apartment, he still hasn't moved back into the zoo. Would you?

Introduction: Walking on Air

Supervisor Terrence Hallinan is seriously proposing to legalize prostitution in San Francisco because it's always been there anyway, isn't going away, can't be effectively policed, and is more trouble while unregulated than it would be if legalized and taxed. The financially strapped civic budget could well use the monetary boost of a hooker's tax, and the sex workers' union, COYOTE, is fully behind the repeal of all criminal laws against prostitution. No other city in California or anywhere but Nevada, has legalized sex for pay, but San Francisco could be the pioneer, again.

If you're gay and in a long-term relationship, San Francisco is definitely the place to live. The 1990 census data showed same-sex households abound in the City, at a ratio practically ten times higher than in New York City and higher even than in West Hollywood, Key West, Palm Springs, or Provincetown.

There's a serious, even urgent, need for public toilets in San Francisco. With all private rest rooms locked or otherwise unavailable, the homeless and desperate have no alternative but to relieve themselves on the streets. As a result, San Francisco stinks, in its hardest-hit quarters.

The tiny town of Colma, only ten miles south of the city line, is San Francisco's cemetery, the place designated to bury the dead. Two to three million deceased occupy the village—nobody knows exactly how many—compared to only eleven hundred living citizens. But here reside the great spirits of the City. William Randolph Hearst is in an unmarked tomb containing a half-full bottle of Evian water. His neighbor is Wyatt Earp. In 1937, San Francisco dug up and moved every grave within the city limits to allow land for economic expansion.

Now where land and sea meet, all comes apart and yet together for San Francisco. Now her secrets can be told. The most scandalous episodes of the past seem only harmless fantasies in our age of casual obscenity. What is confidential is now public, what is hidden is revealed. She is an old whore who's seen everything, but somehow something new keeps coming along.

If you've ever seen the dreamy Golden Gate Bridge from the morning-misted Sausalito ferry, stretching and beckoning you into the wily City; if you read Armistead Maupin's *Tales of the City*, a saucy fiction based on reality, and laughed at the whimsy and charm of it; if you left your heart in some Italian grotto in North Beach and forgot about tomorrow, or lived the dream of social equality in some Berkeley commune, or wandered the foothills or Mill Valley and Marin; if you wondered what went on behind closed doors in San Francisco, and on her rainbow streets: read on.

The Barbary Coast

In 1849, the *New York Evening Post* reported that "the people of San Francisco are mad, stark mad." Thus began a popular perception of the residents of Baghdad by the Bay as seen by Easterners. It's fair to say that many people who don't live in San Francisco still think people who do are crazy—or eccentric, at least.

The madness started with the Gold Rush of 1849, the year that San Francisco became the hottest spot on the American map. The city was originally called Yuerba Buena ("good herb," a telling portent for its underground marijuana culture) but adopted the name San Francisco on January 30, 1847. Captain John A. Sutter and James W. Marshall first discovered gold in the Sacramento River valley in 1848. By 1849, more than fifty thousand prospectors had poured through the Golden Gate. Hopeful gold diggers from Maine to Missouri packed up their belongings and endured the grueling cross-country overland journey to get their share of imagined riches. Vessels sailed into port from every part of the world.

Many ships were simply abandoned in the harbor, all their crew having dashed off to the gold panning fields. Some of these derelict boats were turned into makeshift brothels and hotels. The city population in 1850 was officially twenty-five thousand single men (most under the age of forty) and only three hundred women, mostly prostitutes from Mexico, Peru, and Chile. The latter were called Chileños or "greasers." During the first six months of 1850, more than two thousand new prostitutes arrived in San Francisco from France, New York, and New Orleans to service the insatiable sexual appetites of the gold miners.

The City was born in anarchy. Rampant inflation produced exorbitant prices for housing and all services, and even fresh vegetables and fruit were commodities worth their weight in gold. "Owing almost entirely to the influx of goldseekers and the horde of gamblers, thieves,

A Gay Nineties bar. (*Bettmann*)

harlots, politicians, and other felonious parasites, there arose a unique criminal district that for almost seventy years was the scene of more viciousness and depravity, but which at the same time possessed more glamor, than any other area of vice and iniquity on the American continent," wrote historian Herbert Asbury in 1933.

At least several hundred gambling places were operating in San Francisco by 1850, and in 1855 the City licensed the casinos even though they were prohibited by California state laws. Nobody in San Francisco paid any attention to state law, which was unenforceable anyway. The aptly named Colonel Jack Gamble, a leading proprietor of some of the most popular casinos, commenced a "funny name game" in San Francisco, which the legendary *Chronicle* columnist Herb Caen has kept going into the 1990s. Madame Simone Jules, a strikingly beautiful French woman, became the City's first female roulette dealer in 1850. Fortunes gathered from the gold pan were lost overnight to corrupt gambling tycoons. Gold was the currency of choice, and many a miner arrived in town with heavy pockets only to wake up in a gutter, battered and robbed.

The Hounds, a.k.a. the San Francisco Society of Regulators, were a gang of thugs, killers, and thieves who regularly attacked the Chileños and Mexicans. They were opposed by the notorious outlaw Joaquín Murieta from Sonora, Mexico, who with his band of cutthroats killed many Hounds and others in San Francisco.

British convicts who had been exiled to Australia were occasionally delivered by boat to San Francisco Bay and formed their own criminal gangs called Sydney Ducks or Sydney Coves, operating out of a neighborhood called SydneyTown in the Barbary Coast, an area bordered roughly by Broadway, Washington, Montgomery, and Stockton streets. Among their vile and famous dens were the Boar's Head, where a woman and a boar engaged in sexual congress for an audience; the Goat and Compass, where a character known as Dirty Tom McAlear would for a small fee eat or drink any kind of excrement (until he was finally arrested on the charge of "making a beast of himself"); and the Fierce Grizzly, where an actual bear wrestled with men, and even the milk was spiked with gin.

Nobody was safe on the streets of the Barbary Coast, whether by night or day. The police, as few as they were, took bribes from the

The Barbary Coast, 1912, when prostitution was still legal in "Baghdad by the Bay." (*Bettmann*)

criminals themselves and generally feared to go there. Prosecutions were rare, convictions almost nonexistent. The whole place was ruled by anarchic force, chaos, and bedlam.

The noncriminal population of San Francisco finally got fed up and formed a vigilante posse to take the law into their own hands. The notorious SydneyTown criminal John Jenkins, "the Miscreant," who led a bloody career of murder and thievery, was lynched on June 10, 1851, by the newly formed Committee of Vigilance. A little more than a month later, on July 11, they hanged the famously evil English Jim on Market Street wharf, and on August 24 Sydney Ducks Samuel Whittaker and Robert McKenzie were hanged. For a time, the Australian convict population fled in terror to the gold panning areas.

But the city fathers, including the corrupt mayor David C. Broderick,

Western terminus of the California Railroad Company at Presidio and California streets, circa 1883. (*Bettmann*)

objected to rule by lynch mob, and the Committee of Vigilance was disbanded. By 1855, the criminals were back, in even more flagrant disregard for the law than ever. "Masked men appeared openly in the streets and garrotted citizens, defying law or resistance. Politics was in fact accountable for this chaotic condition of city affairs. Ballot box stuffing placed men in office. The town was ruled by gamblers, rowdies, and state prison convicts. Sydney Ducks again were cackling in the pond," wrote J. W. Buel in *Metropolitan Life Unveiled.*

A second vigilante committee gathered in 1856 after the popular crusading journalist James King was shot by a Broderick supporter and City Hall crony, James P. Casey. City authorities gave in to the lynch mob and surrendered Casey from the city jail, and he was paraded through the streets of the Barbary Coast and hanged. On June 3, 1856, California governor J. Neely Johnson issued a proclamation declaring San Francisco to be in a "state of insurrection."

The Barbary Coast grew and expanded its boundaries as houses of prostitution, saloons, and gambling places became the essence of San Francisco's social structure and the foundation for the city's continuing reputation as a sordid hotbed of crime, sex, and murder. The Barbary Coast was synonymous with debauchery and danger. The *San Francisco Call* in 1869 described it as "that sink of moral pollution, whose reefs are strewn with human wrecks, that home of vice and harbor of destruction, the coast on which no gentle breezes blow, but where rages one wild sirocco of sin!" Pacific Street from the ocean west to Kearney Street was one solid, densely packed avenue of dance halls, melodeons, cheap groggeries, wine and beer dens known as deadfalls, and concert saloons.

"Pretty waiter girls," some as young as twelve or thirteen and all sexually experienced, wore gaudy costumes and flirted with the customers, almost universally male. For fifty cents, a man could strip any girl of his fancy and view her nude. A seedy dive called the Bull Run employed forty to fifty of the most abandoned, hopeless, abused women on the Barbary Coast, who were forced to drink real liquor (better places gave their prostitutes tea in place of whiskey) and then were raped by dozens of men while unconscious. The price of having intercourse with such a pathetic victim ran from twenty-five cents to a dollar, with an extra charge of twenty-five cents for watching other men victimize the girl.

Alcohol wasn't the only ingestible vice on the Barbary Coast, of course. Cocaine and morphine were both popular and widely available. In 1879, a place perfectly named The Morgue was headquarters for the district's drug addicts. Kearney and California streets comprised a famous deadfall known for its waitresses dressed in tiny skirts and silk stockings, but nothing above the waist. They initiated the topless dancing tradition that Carol Doda revived in North Beach almost a century later, in the 1950s. The most popular strip shows in the Barbary Coast were at the Bella Union hall, a legally licensed emporium of legitimate vaudeville theater and gambling.

By 1890, San Francisco had licensed 3,117 drinking establishments, or one for every ninety-six residents, with at least another two thousand illegal speakeasies (called "blind pigs") known to be in business. Never in the history of the City, including today, has there been such a high ratio of bars to population, but San Francisco is still a drinking person's town in every way.

Western Town With Eastern Manners

San Francisco's world-renowned Chinatown also belonged to the Barbary Coast and sprang from the insanity of the Gold Rush days. Chinese immigration to the Golden Gate began in 1848, just after the first discovery of gold, and peaked in 1870. Wah Lee opened the first Chinese laundry in 1851, and it was quickly followed by dozens of others as the miners were willing to pay princely sums to have their clothing washed, a service previously unavailable in the City.

The discrimination and hatred leveled against the Chinese immigrants was ugly in the extreme. Virtually the entire white population felt it was perfectly all right to bash any Chinese man or woman. Leland Stanford, governor of California from 1861 to 1863, was publicly prejudiced, announcing that "the presence of numbers of that degraded and distinct people would exercise a deleterious effect upon the superior race." He didn't announce that he also secretly imported thousands of Chinese laborers to build his Central Pacific Railroad.

Conditions in Chinatown were deplorable. People lived five hundred to a huge room at the underground cellar dubbed in jest the Palace Hotel. In 1868, a criminal youth gang emerged that specialized in public riots aimed against the Chinese. These vicious criminals were called Hoodlums, from their habit of warning "Huddle 'em!" when in danger. Their attacks led to indiscriminate violence against the immigrants.

The king of the Hoodlums was James Riley, who had an exceptionally large penis and sold photos of himself in the nude for fifty cents. He used his thick head to butt holes in doors and attack enemies. His chief cohort was Billy Smith, leader of the widely feared Valley Boys, or Rising Star Club, an unscrupulous gang of two hundred hardened street boys.

Chinatown offered the white population of the Barbary Coast the new diversions of opium dens and legal slave trading. The opium dens were patronized by the City's aristocrats as safe places where they could get high without fear. "Yellow" prostitution in fact remained legal in San Francisco until 1914. In the 1870s the *Chronicle* referred to the "importation of females in bulk." The "lookee" fee (for looking at naked women) was usually twenty-five cents, but a dollar for the finest and as little as a dime in the low dives. Girls posed in "cribs" on the street, chanting, "Two bittee lookee, four bittee feelee, six bittee doee." Disease was widespread in these girls, and in turn it spread to the general population.

The system of Chinese prostitution was based in slave ownership. Girls were bought in China for around eighty dollars, from parents who considered female children a nuisance and were more than willing to sell them. Once brought into San Francisco, such a girl was worth $400 to $1,000 depending on her youth and beauty.

The girls were literally auctioned off in Chinatown. Once the price was established, it was paid (usually in gold) into the girl's hands, and she turned the money over to the man who had sold her, while signing a contract that read: "For the consideration of (whatever sum) paid into my hands this day, I (name) promise to prostitute my body for the term of (number of) years. If, in that time, I am sick one day, two weeks shall be added to my time; and if more than one day, my term of prostitution shall continue an additional month. But if I run away or escape from the custody of my keeper, then I am to be held as a slave for life. (Signed.)"

Of course the point of the "sick day" provision was that every month the girl would have a menstrual period, which would render her ineligible for prostitution and also extend her slavery a month. Many of these poor creatures never lived to see their freedom.

Shanghaied Away

Chinese prostitutes were not the only human commodity on the Barbary Coast. Sailors were often "shanghaied" into service against their will. (In fact, the verb *to Shanghai*, or to steal someone's body and put it on a boat, was invented in San Francisco. There were no direct shipping connections between San Francisco and Shanghai, so sailors who made that crossing had to travel around the world. Thus any long and dangerous journey came to be known as a shanghai.)

Any able-bodied sailor could be drugged or knocked out with a sleeping potion in his drink, and his body carried by night onto an

A quiet day on the Barbary Coast, "the Wickedest Street in the World," in San Francisco's less licentious phase of 1957.
(*AP/Wide World Photos*)

outgoing ship in the harbor. By the time the poor fellow woke up, he was on his way to some distant land and under the whip of a scurrilous captain. Professional kidnappers carried out these human heists for a fee per body, and sometimes dead bodies or even stuffed dummies were substituted for live sailors. Many murders in San Francisco were never solved because the corpse had been shipped off to sea as a live sailor.

Doom and Destruction of the Barbary Coast

By 1906, the uptown Tenderloin in the Barbary Coast housed the first male brothel in San Francisco, where handsome young men were

offered for sexual favors at the enormous price of ten dollars an evening. Thus began the history of available male prostitutes in the City
by the Bay, and simultaneously down came the wrath of nature in a
hideous calamity many believed to be the work of God smashing
America's own Sodom and Gomorrah. That event, of course, was the
April 18, 1906, great earthquake and subsequent fire that utterly destroyed the Barbary Coast neighborhood.

Suffering and devastation were everywhere. The entire district had
to be rebuilt from the ground up, and naturally new saloons and dens
of vice immediately appeared. But the legendary Sin City never again
reached the depths of its previous excesses. By 1913, William Randolph Hearst's paper, the *Examiner*, attacked the Barbary Coast and
called for its abolition. And in 1914, the California legislature passed
the Red Light Abatement Act, formally ending legal prostitution in San
Francisco.

But the twentieth-century reforms couldn't change the historic path
that San Francisco had set out upon. The new city might not be as
dangerous and evil as the old Barbary Coast, but sex, drugs, alcohol,
gambling, robbery, and murder were well entrenched as traditions—
and have remained so.

Dining on the Edge of the World?

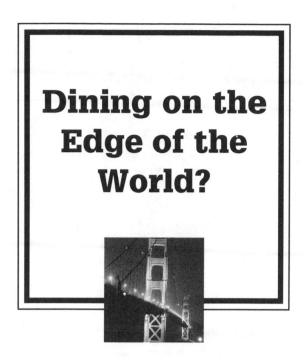

Luna's Mexican restaurant has no address. It is on no particular street, at no particular corner, even its habitués, its most enthusiastic devotees, are unable to locate it on demand. It is "over there in the quarter," "not far from the cathedral there." One could find it if one started out with that intent; but to direct another there—no, that is out of the question. It *can* be reached by following the alleys of Chinatown. You will come out of the last alley—the one where the slave girls are—upon the edge of the Mexican quarter, and by going ahead for a block or two, and by keeping a sharp lookout to the right and left you will hit upon it. It is always to be searched for. Always to be discovered.

—NOVELIST FRANK NORRIS, 1890

The reason San Francisco became so famous for its food dates back to the 1870s and 1880s, when rich industrialists arrived in town in private railroad cars, bringing with them their own hired chefs. As often as not, these *chefs de cuisine* stayed behind in the City, providing elegant meals to a population eager and ready to pay large sums for gourmet cooking on the wild frontier.

By 1890, three French restaurants in particular had become well established. They were the Maison Riche, the Maison Dorée, and the Poulet d'Or, or golden chicken, which featured a gilt-leaf sculpture of a chicken over its door. Since the miners couldn't pronounce Poulet d'Or properly, they called it the Poodle Dog, and so it was known for years.

Typically, the fine restaurants also had upstairs dining rooms, equipped with a sofa and completely private. Gentlemen could bring their whores to dine via a side entrance in the alley that led directly to the second floor. This was called a "carriage entrance."

The Luna's Mexican restaurant that Frank Norris wrote about was on Telegraph Hill, at the intersection that is now Grant Avenue and Vallejo Street. It had Victorian lace curtains, an ornate parlor, and red-and-white checked tablecloths and was the original of today's North Beach bistros, with a highly artistic and literary clientele, oceans of red wine, and a bohemian menu of fiery tamales and enchiladas for twenty-five cents a meal. The enormous proprietor, Riccardo, was sometimes known to accept a painting or short story in lieu of cash from a hungry "regular" diner.

It remained for a place called Warner's Cobweb Palace to introduce the San Francisco tradition of a restaurant on a pier (Meigg's Wharf in North Beach) that served only seafood and sourdough bread. House specialties included cracked crab, clam chowder, and mussels. The decor featured all sorts of bric-a-brac transported from far-off lands to the port of San Francisco—totem poles from Alaska, masks from China and Japan, war clubs from the South Seas. And the bar was famed for the high quality of its drinks, especially for genuine French brandy.

Ordinary people, however, found their sustenance at corner saloons, which competed with each other in laying out free buffets of extravagant hors d'oeuvres, effectively giving birth to the now traditional happy hour, in which the purchase of a drink entitled the patron to eat limitlessly without paying. In New York, this became known as the free lunch. But it was nowhere as good as in San Francisco around 1900, where the complimentary goodies included caviar, imported cheeses, salmon, Virginia ham baked in brandy, shrimp in crème de

Dining on the Edge of the World?

menthe, pork, lamb, roast beef, cabbage, diamondback terrapin, sweetbreads, pears, venison, clams, and oysters on the half shell.

Today's San Francisco happy hour, alas, may be nothing but pretzels and peanuts unless you're drinking at the Top of the Mark or some place where the drinks cost as much as a meal once did. But the sourdough bread, ah! It's as good as ever.

Mark Twain in San Francisco

The great earthquake of October 8, 1865, left a strong impression on young journalist Samuel Clemens (Mark Twain), who made the famous remark that the coldest winter he had ever suffered was a summer in San Francisco. Here is an excerpt from his "Earthquake Almanac" as published in the *Daily Dramatic Chronicle*:

At the insistence of several friends who feel a boding anxiety to know beforehand what sort of phenomena we may expect the elements to exhibit during the next month or two, and who have lost all confidence in the various patent medicine almanacs, because of the unaccountable reticence of those works concerning the extraordinary event of the 8th inst., I have compiled the following almanac expressly for this latitude:

Oct. 17—Weather hazy; atmosphere murky and dense. An expression of profound melancholy will be observable on most countenances.

Oct. 18—Slight earthquake. Countenances grow more melancholy.

Mark Twain in San Francisco

Mark Twain once remarked that the coldest winter he had ever spent was a summer in San Francisco. (*Bettmann*)

Oct. 19—Look out for rain. It will be absurd to look in for it. The general depression of spirits increased.

Oct. 20—More weather.

Oct. 21—Same.

Oct. 22—Light winds, perhaps. If they blow, it will be from the "east'ard, or the nor'ard, or the west'ard, or the suth'ard," or from some general direction approximating more or less to these points of the compass or otherwise. Winds are uncertain—more especially when they blow from whence they cometh and whither they listeth. N.B.—Such is the nature of winds.

Oct. 23—Mild, balmy earthquakes.

Oct. 24—Shaky.

Oct. 25—Occasional shakes, followed by light showers of bricks and plastering. N.B.—Stand from under.

Oct. 26—Considerable phenomenal atmospheric foolishness. About this time expect more earthquakes, but do not look out for them, on account of the bricks.

Oct. 27—Universal despondency, indicative of approaching disaster. Abstain from smiling, or indulgence in humorous conversation, or exasperating jokes.

Oct. 28—Misery, dismal forebodings and despair. Beware of all discourse—a joke uttered at this time would produce a popular outbreak.

Oct. 29—Beware!

Oct. 30—Keep dark!

Oct. 31—Go slow!

Nov. 1—Terrific earthquake. This is the great earthquake month. More stars fall and more worlds are slathered around carelessly and destroyed in November than in any other month of the twelve.

Nov. 2—Spasmodic but exhilarating earthquakes, accompanied by occasional showers of rain, and churches and things.

Nov. 3—Make your will.

Nov. 4—Sell out.

Nov. 5—Select your "last words." Those of John Quincy Adams will do, with the addition of a syllable thus: "This is the last of earthquakes."

Nov. 6—Prepare to shed this mortal coil.

Nov. 7—Shed.

Nov. 8—The sun will rise as usual, perhaps; but if he does he will doubtless be staggered some to find nothing but a large round hole eight thousand miles in diameter in the place where he saw this world serenely spinning the day before.

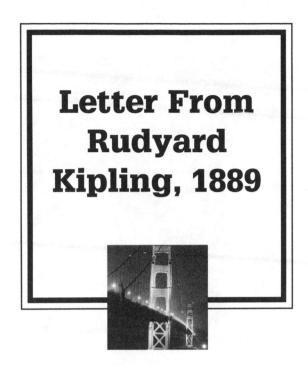

Letter From Rudyard Kipling, 1889

Protect me from the wrath of an outraged community if these letters be ever read by American eyes. San Francisco is a mad city—inhabited for the most part by perfectly insane people whose women are of a remarkable beauty. When the "City of Peking" steamed through the Golden Gate I saw with great joy that the block-house which guarded the mouth of the "finest harbour in the world, Sir," could be silenced by two gunboats from Hong Kong with safety, comfort and dispatch.

Then a reporter leaped aboard, and ere I could gasp held me in his toils. He pumped me exhaustively while I was getting ashore, demanding, of all things in the world, news about Indian journalism. It is an awful thing to enter a new land with a new lie on your lips. I spoke the truth to the evil-minded Custom-house man who turned my most sacred raiment on a floor composed of stable-refuse and pine-splinters; but the reporter overwhelmed me not so much by his poignant audacity as his beautiful ignorance. I am sorry now that I did not tell him more lies as I passed into a city of three hundred thousand white men! Think of it! Three hundred thousand white men and women gathered in one spot, walking upon real pavements in front of real plate-glass windowed

Rudyard Kipling found San Francisco a bizarre and dangerous place.
(*AP/Wide World Photos*)

*shops, and talking something that was not very different from English.
It was only when I had tangled myself up in a hopeless maze of small
wooden houses, dust, street-refuse, and children who play with empty
kerosene tins, that I discovered the difference of speech.*

*"You want to go to the Palace Hotel?" said an affable youth on a
dray. "What in hell are you doing here, then? This is about the lowest
place in the city. Go six blocks north to corner of Geary and Market; then
walk around till you strike corner of Sutter and Sixteeth, and that brings
you there."*

*I do not vouch for the literal accuracy of these directions, quoting but
from a disordered memory.*

*"Amen," I said. "But who am I that I should strike the corners of such
as you name? Peradventure they be gentlemen of repute, and might hit
back. Bring it down to dots, my son."*

*He explained that no one ever used the word "street," and that every
one was supposed to know how the streets run; for sometimes the names
were upon the lamps and sometimes they weren't. Fortified with these*

Letter From Rudyard Kipling, 1889

directions I proceeded till I found a mighty street full of sumptuous build-ings four or five stories high, but paved with rude cobble stones in the fashion of the Year One. A cable-car without any visible means of support slid stealthily behind me and nearly struck me in the back. A hundred yards further there was a slight commotion in the street. A pon-derous Irish gentleman with priest's cords in his hat and a small nickel-plated badge on his fat bosom emerged from the knot, supporting a Chinaman who had been stabbed in the eye and was bleeding like a pig. The bystanders went their ways and the Chinaman, assisted by the policeman, his own. Of course this was none of my business, but I rather wanted to know what had happened to the gentleman who had dealt the stab.

There were no more incidents till I reached the Palace Hotel, a seven storied warren of humanity with a thousand rooms in it. All the travel books will tell you about hotel arrangements in this country. They should be seen to be appreciated. Understand clearly—and this letter is written after a thousand miles of experiences—that money will not buy you service in the West.

When the hotel clerk—the man who awards your room to you and who is supposed to give you information—when that resplendent indi-vidual stoops to attend to your wants, he does so whistling or humming, or picking his teeth, or pauses to converse with someone he knows. These performances, I gather, are to impress upon you that he is a free man and your equal. From his general appearance and the size of his diamonds he ought to be your superior.

No man rose to tell me what were the lions of the place. No one volunteered any sort of conveyance. I was absolutely alone in this big city of white folks. By instinct I sought refreshment and came upon a bar-room, full of bad Salon pictures, in which men with hats on the backs of their heads were wolfing food from a counter. It was the institution of the "free lunch," that I had struck. You paid for a drink and got as much as you wanted to eat. For something less than a rupee a day, a man can feed himself sumptuously in San Francisco, even though he be bankrupt. Remember this if ever you are stranded in these parts.

Later, I began a vast but unsystematic exploration of the streets. I asked for no names. It was enough that the pavements were full of white men and women, the streets clanging with traffic, and that the restful roar of a

Powell Street cable cars, 1901. (*Bettman*)

great city rang in my ears. The cable-cars glided to all points of the compass. I took them one by one until I could go no further. San Francisco has been pitched down on the sand-bunkers of the Bikaneer desert. About one-fourth of it is ground reclaimed-from the sea—any old timer will tell you about that. The remainder is ragged, unthrifty sand-hills, pegged down by houses.

From an English point of view there has not been the least attempt at grading those hills, and indeed you might as well try to grade the hillocks of Sind. The cable-cars have for all practical purposes made San Francisco a dead level. They take no count of rise or fall, but slide equably on their appointed courses from one end to the other of a six-mile street. They turn corners almost at right angles; cross other lines, and for aught I know, may run up the sides of houses. There is no visible agency of their flight; but once in a while you shall pass a five storied building, humming with machinery that winds up an everlasting wire-cable, and the initiated will tell you that here is the mechanism. I gave up asking questions. If it pleases Providence to make a car run up and down a slit in the ground for many miles, and if for two pence halfpenny I can ride in that car, why shall I seek reasons of the miracle?

Quake City

There had been strong earthquakes in 1865, and again in 1868, but the developers of San Francisco, with the notable exception of William Ralston and his Palace Hotel, paid them no mind. The City was simply thrown up on landfill along Market and Mission streets and the port without regard to seismic safety. The notoriously steep hills were jammed with flimsy buildings cheek by jowl. Even the $6 million City Hall completed around the turn of the century was more grandiose than safe.

So when the great earthquake hit in the early morning of April 18, 1906, San Francisco was helplessly vulnerable. Hundreds of buildings just plain fell down, collapsing on top of other buildings and filling the streets with rubble. The walls and great stone columns of City Hall tumbled down like Jericho's, leaving its ornate dome delicately balanced on a wildly unsafe foundation.

This vision has remained with us throughout the century as the definition of what an earthquake is and the destruction it represents. People who have never experienced an earthquake think of San Francisco in terms of Quake City, even if Los Angeles and Tokyo are no less dangerous.

Few buildings in San Francisco of 1906 were constructed to withstand
an earthquake. (*Bettmann*)

But the greatest damage of the 1906 quake came not from the shaking itself but from the fire that followed. San Francisco was completely unequipped to deal with the sweeping conflagration that took the City down in flames. The previous year, 1905, the National Board of Fire Underwriters had warned that San Francisco's water capacity of thirty-six million gallons a day would not be enough to cope with a truly major fire. The City's Board of Supervisors ignored that report and every plea from the fire department for more and better preparations.

One of the first casualties of the quake was the central fire station on Brenham Place in Chinatown, near North Beach. Other firehouses were also in shambles, and the horses needed to pull the fire engines were hysterical and running amok. Even when a horse-drawn fire truck

More destructive than the earthquake of 1906 was the fire that tore
through the city in its wake. (*Bettmann*)

could reach the scene of a blaze through the rubble-strewn streets, there wasn't enough water pressure to extinguish the burning. People just had to stand by and watch San Francisco burn to the ground. Sixty percent of the City went up in smoke.

People weren't prepared for the fire. They seemed to believe, once the shaking had stopped, that those buildings still standing would be spared. But on the day after the quake, and for three days running, underground dynamite explosions and wind-fanned flames leveled the metropolis that had been thrown up so quickly and carelessly.

The aforementioned William Ralston and his Palace Hotel, however, provided graphic evidence to San Francisco that precautions taken at great expense really paid off in the end. The hotel survived the quake and fire with only some cracked marble and shattered glass, but no important structural collapse. Built in 1876 at the staggering cost of $5 million, the Palace had brick walls two feet thick, twelve-foot-deep foundation pillars, and three thousand tons of iron bands welded into one continuous girdle to make the building as safe as possible in an earthquake.

Free Radicals

As if the mystic Bay itself spawned strange creatures from some other planet, San Francisco has always proved a hospitable place for kooks, nuts, new movements, revolutions, social change, and cults. Jim Jones and his People's Temple sprang out of this environment, following the example of history. Werner Erhard launched his est seminars here, the latest in a long string of far-out belief systems.

You have to go back to the Gold Rush days of crazed, anarchic young men running amok in its streets to see how San Francisco readily adapts to any suggestion. A fellow named Emperor Norton proclaimed himself the royal ruler of the city and was cordially greeted by his loyal subjects. The editors of the *Chronicle* were occasionally shot by readers irate over something that appeared in print. (Even today, you can't get into the *Chronicle* Building without security clearance.) Zen Buddhism and Taoism, once considered exotic, alien religions, got their first American movements underway in the Bay Area.

In the 1950s, the Beatniks launched a second-half-of-the-twentieth-century resurgence in San Franciscan notoriety. Once word got out, hipsters and swingers from all over the country descended on the

North Beach neighborhood, where Lawrence Ferlinghetti opened his City Lights bookstore and *On the Road* novelist Jack Kerouac burned brightly.

(Except he didn't really. Kerouac spent some months in San Francisco and wrote about the experience extensively, so he came to be associated with the City. But his time spent there was a relatively small part of his life, and after sundering himself from the Beats and returning to Lowell, Massachusetts, to live with his mother, he never came back to the Bay.)

The Beatniks were the parents of the following generation, the Hippies. Both groups got started in San Francisco. In the '50s, the country was complacently united behind President Eisenhower and the Cold War against Russia, and along came these beaten-up characters, "cats" with goatees and "chicks" with long, stringy hair, poets who smoked marijuana cigarettes and recited their howling, angry verse in coffeehouses, musicians who pounded bongo drums, rebels without a cause, nihilists.

They became a kind of cartoon to straight Americans. The TV situation comedy "The Many Loves of Dobie Gillis" featured a Beatnik sidekick named Maynard G. Krebs. They espoused "free love." They stood for nothing, but they represented something very real. They were for nonconformity, for the right to be different, to reject the zeitgeist of Plastic America.

In 1957, ('57 Heaven), Kerouac published *On the Road* and Allen Ginsberg his seminal poem, "Howl." Both are still required reading for almost every college student. The national media descended on San Francisco, eager to get the inside story. Publicity spoiled the scene, of course, and the true Beats retreated under the onslaught of tourists, wannabes, curiosity seekers, and journalists and scholars studying the phenomenon.

The Beatniks were never very political or demonstrative, unlike the Hippies who followed them. Being Beat was of itself a kind of politics of indifference. You went to the coffeehouse, you smoked cigarettes, you "scored" with "chicks" in lofts, but actually doing anything to change society was, like, square. You wrote, painted, or made music, *that* was doing something.

"Jack Kerouac opened a million coffee bars and sold a million Levis to both sexes," said Beat novelist William S. Burroughs many years

Free Radicals

When not on the road, Jack Kerouac frequented the City Lights bookshop in San Francisco. (*Bettmann*)

later. In the Beats' time, the favorite hangouts in North Beach were the Co-Existence Bagel Shop and the Bread and Wine Mission, plus a groovy place called The Place. These joints were regularly busted and closed by the police on flimsy charges of public nuisance, but they always reopened. Poetry cannot be shackled in San Francisco.

This was proven again in 1993, when the City ultimately backed off on its attempt to impose an "entertainment" tax on poetry readings in public coffeehouses. The poetry community exploded in protest.

Let's face it, poetry readings are *not* entertainment. In the Mission District today, there are places that lure you into the back room for a poetry reading, after loosening you up with cheap wine or perhaps a joint, and next thing you know, *you can't leave*. Not without offending the poets, that is. The many poets, waiting to read you their work . . .

Jack Kerouac himself said, "Maybe the Beat Generation, which is the offspring of the Lost Generation, is just another step toward that last, pale generation which will not know the answer, either."

The next step was taken by the Hippies and Radicals of the '60s. They were two different groups, with a great deal of relationship and movement back and forth over the line. The Radicals took over Berkeley with their causes: civil rights, peace, and academic revolution. The Hippies took over San Francisco with theirs: hedonism and cosmic inspiration.

In both cases, the Bay Area led the nation and the world. College kids in other parts of the country looked to Berkeley for examples of how to shake up the system. All kinds of kids, and even some adults, looked to the Haight Ashbury communal Hippie lifestyle as a harbinger of a New Age.

Lawrence Ferlinghetti (left, rear) looks on as two professors peddle a banned book of poetry at his City Lights bookshop, 1966. (*Bettmann*)

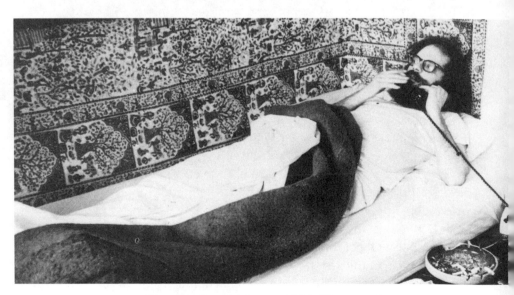

Allen Ginsberg at home, 1966. (*Bettmann*)

Empress
Dianne the
First

When Dianne Feinstein was mayor of San Francisco and greeted Queen Elizabeth of England upon Her Majesty's arrival in the town, people said it was hard to tell which of the ladies was more regal. They were equally aristocratic, and Dianne was a hell of a lot taller (six feet in heels).

When you consider her background, it's easy to believe that this particular wealthy Pacific Heights matron, now a U.S. senator, could hardly be fazed by meeting a mere royal personage. Feinstein could easily be president of the United States and it would only be an after-thought to her terms as mayor, anointed in blood. On the same day in 1975 that she announced her intended retirement from politics, she wound up kneeling on the floor of City Hall with her fingers plunged into the bullet holes Dan White left in Mayor George Moscone. So much for retirement. As president of the Board of Supervisors, on his death she became mayor.

Her life has also been touched by mental illness, divorce, death, humiliating political defeats, financial scandals, you name it, yet she always seems to emerge unflustered and in control. Born in San Fran-

Tony Bennett, who immortalized San Francisco in song, and Dianne Feinstein kick off a civic celebration, 1984. (*Bettmann*)

cisco in 1934 to a prominent family, she grew up in a kind of private hell. Her mother, Betty, was brain-damaged and alcoholic, suicidal and sometimes violent. Dianne and her sisters were often beaten. Her father, a noted surgeon and professor named Leon Goldman, used to have to force Betty to vomit up the sleeping pills she downed. While the outside world saw the Goldman family as rich and proper, Dianne's life was filled with misery and instability.

She went to Stanford and excelled, getting elected to the office of student body vice president (at a time when the president was always a boy, the vice president a girl). She married young, but disastrously, and at age twenty-four was divorced with a small child, an insidious disadvantage for someone with political ambitions. But she did have some connections to City Hall through her Uncle Morris, and eventually she convinced California governor Pat Brown to appoint her to a parole board for women prisoners in the state. Thus began a tortuous climb.

Her second marriage was to Bertram Feinstein, a brain surgeon. She got elected to the Board of Supervisors in 1969, certainly using some of her husband's influence and money, but she was badly defeated in two attempts to win the mayor's office. Dr. Feinstein eventually died of cancer, as Dianne's father also had done, following a long and tormented illness, and once again Dianne had to go it solo.

Her third husband, Richard Blum, was and is a financier whose international investments and lavish lifestyle led to many unsubstan-

Feinstein at a press conference regarding the jury's decision on Dan White, 1979. (*Bettmann*)

Feinstein talks with the press the day after she defeated an incumbent
for the Senate seat, 1992. (*Bettmann*)

tiated charges of financial misconduct; he became a new sugar daddy
to underwrite her political career. Always poised and elegant, "tough
but caring" (her own slogan), Dianne won several tumultuous terms
in charge of the City before deciding to run for governor in 1990. She

didn't win, falling by the narrowest of margins to Republican Pete Wilson, but two years later the Democratic sweep that put Bill Clinton in the White House took her and Barbara Boxer to the U.S. Senate from California.

While running for re-election to the Senate in 1994, Dianne has even enjoyed the financial and logistical support of some leading Republicans—oh, the horror and shame. Former GOP congressman and staunch conservative Robert Lagomarsino has been actively working for the Feinstein campaign against Santa Barbara Republican Michael Huffington, who is thoroughly loathed by some of his own party members. Practical gal that she is, Dianne has welcomed the crossover support while retaining her trademark independence.

Gun Crazy

People in California bought six hundred thousand in 1993. The Rodney King riots in L.A. did wonders for the already thriving firearms business as people realized the police simply couldn't protect them. In the Bay Area, Oakland is the principal center of the gun trade, and it's as easy to buy an assault rifle as a ticket to the Golden State Warriors basketball game.

So it came as a surprise when the San Francisco Board of Supervisors went after the one and only "real" gun dealer in the City, the fifty-year-old San Francisco Gun Exchange, which sells firearms to the police themselves, has a sterling record of refusing to do business with criminals, and doesn't even stock assault rifles.

Specifically, the Board levied a 3 percent tax on the gross sales of the Gun Exchange, twice the tax charged to other small businesses in town. The rationale is that guns kill people, but everyone concedes that real criminals will always find a way to buy a gun, no matter the price, and probably won't venture into the almost venerable Gun Exchange.

Brother-and-sister team Bob and Elizabeth Posner inherited the store from their father, Nathan, and operate it almost like a Western museum. "Some of our clientele are the children and grandchildren of our father's clientele," Elizabeth said. Most are hunters, target shooters, or law enforcement personnel. The Police Officers Association teams with the store in giving safety lessons and demonstrations. And the Gun Exchange rigorously screens out bad guys and does background checks on its customers.

"If we thought we were hurting people, we'd get out of this business," said Bob Posner. "Who could live with themselves?" Shades of flower power in the barrel!

Reverend Jim Jones: From San Francisco to Eternity

In 1977, Reverend Jim Jones was the chairman of the San Francisco Housing Authority, a political appointee honored as one of the City's most important people. California governor Jerry Brown made a speech at Jones's church, the People's Temple, with his arm around Jim's shoulder. President Jimmy Carter and his wife, Rosalyn, praised his good work. San Francisco mayors Joe Alioto and George Moscone both spoke at the populist temple, and in 1977 Jim Jones received the City's Martin Luther King Humanitarian Award.

A year later, he presided over the group suicide of 912 people in a forlorn jungle encampment bearing his name. Jonestown was a mass cemetery, a grim ending to an electrifying rise that happened in the ferment of San Francisco in the 1970s. It was a time when the City was willing to believe in saviors.

And then along came Jones. Originally a self-proclaimed prophet and teacher, Jones moved his family from Indiana to Ukiah, California, in 1965, ostensibly to escape racism. He was a faith healer with all the flamboyance of a TV evangelist, who used snooping methods to get background information on his "patients," knowledge that would

1977. Reverend Jim Jones (left), then chairman of the San Francisco Housing Authority and one of the most highly respected people in San Francisco, was widely admired in political circles. Here he shakes hands with Mayor George Moscone (right), who would later present Jones with the City's Martin Luther King Humanitarian Award.
(*AP/Wide World Photos*)

make his healing skills seem more legitimate. Charismatic and domineering, he developed a great following in a relatively short time, especially after moving to San Francisco in 1975.

The People's Temple under Jones's direction allied itself with many causes of the Left and became the darling of the Bay Area's large liberal community. Jones moved with ease among high-ranking Democrats, although his views were considerably more radical than centrist. Nonetheless, when Jones met with Walter Mondale during the 1976 Carter-Mondale presidential campaign, he asked the future vice president pointedly for the ambassadorship to Guyana, in South America, and Mondale replied "You got it." Jones was known for his ability to deliver votes.

The People's Temple congregation was about 80 percent black and included a number of misfits and outcasts, people with criminal records or histories of drug addiction. Jones was famous for his ability to reform incorrigible sinners, making them into productive members of society. His greatest believers devoted their lives and all their energy to his orders.

In the winter of 1976–77, Jim Jones was at the height of his powers in San Francisco. He considered the women of People's Temple his wives, and all their children as his own. And he kidnapped John Victor Stoen, age five, from parents Grace and Tim Stoen after they became disaffected with Jones and quit the temple. Tim Stoen was an assistant district attorney in the City and had once been Jones's chief administrative aide, while Grace Stoen lived with the group and willingly gave her son to "Father" Jim. When they left, however, Jones refused to surrender the child and eventually moved him to Jonestown in Guyana.

Grace Stoen made impassioned efforts to get her son returned to her. She filed lawsuits, begged the authorities for help, made kidnapping charges, all to no avail. Jones had enough political clout and friends in high places to fend off her efforts and retain custody of the boy. Finally, Grace told her story to *San Francisco Chronicle* reporters Marshall Kilduff and Phil Tracy for an interview that appeared in *New West* magazine. People's Temple employed a pattern of intimidation against the L.A.-based magazine to try to stop publication of the article, but when it came out many powerful backers, including Mayor George Moscone, continued to support Jones, saying that the piece contained unproven allegations.

Yet the stories of child beating, torture, fanatical tirades by Jones, and his proclamation of himself as a Messianic supreme being refused to go away. The politics of paranoia were revealed in Jones's visit with exiled Black Panther Huey Newton in Havana, Cuba, in January 1977. Newton was a fugitive from the law in Oakland, wanted on murder charges. Jones used the term "revolutionary suicide" in his conversations with Newton, an idea he'd come to promote with the bodies of his own congregation.

Jones was also a sexual tyrant. Although bisexual himself, he taunted and condemned homosexuals. He said his spiritual energy was so great that he had to masturbate thirty times a day, and many women in the congregation sacrificed themselves to help gratify his insatiable appetites.

With the custody fight over little John Stoen driving him to ranting paranoia, Jones took the core group of a thousand or so true believers to the jungles of Guyana and the shantytown commune called Jonestown. There, he broadcast all-night conspiracy theories over shortwave radio to San Francisco. At one point, he threatened mass suicide if the authorities would not cease in their attempts to retrieve the young boy. He demanded his entire group be given asylum in any socialist country.

Meanwhile, allegations were made that people were being held in Jonestown against their will. Relatives and friends of those living there began asking Bay Area legislators for help in getting their loved ones out. Tom Hayden and Jane Fonda were among those who continued to support Jones. In a letter backing the fiery leader, Fonda said she wanted to "recommit myself to your congregation as an active and full participant, not only for myself but because I want my two children to have the experience."

Northern California congressman Leo Ryan stepped into this controversy with a promise to visit Jones in Guyana and personally escort back to San Francisco any residents of Jonestown who wished to leave. A few residents did go with him, but Ryan and four others were ambushed and shot to death by Jones loyalists as they tried to board their plane at the Port Kaituma airport on November 18, 1978.

That evening, Jones led his 912 sheep to the slaughter in a group ingestion of cyanide-laced Kool-Aid punch. The babies were killed first, with squirts of punch from eyedroppers and syringes. Jones himself was found with a bullet hole in his head, but it was never determined whether he killed himself or had someone else do it. All of San Francisco and the nation grieved over the almost unbelievable death toll.

Hundreds of the dead went unclaimed—especially the children. Little John Victor Stoen was among four hundred bodies buried in a mass grave at Evergreen Cemetery in Oakland. Many were never even identified. Fifteen years later, the daughter of one of the victims,

The grim truth: The publisher of the *San Francisco Examiner* holds up the front page of the paper's November 20, 1978 edition. (*Bettmann*)

Jynona Norwood, is raising funds to construct a Vietnam Veterans–type memorial wall, bearing the names of all the people who died at Jonestown. Except one—Jim Jones.

From the streets of San Francisco to an agricultural commune devoted to the ideals of socialism and racial equality, the People's Temple offered a dream that many people admired but turned into a nightmare that left the world gasping in disbelief. Only San Francisco could have nurtured its eccentric growth and given Jim Jones the cachet of leadership and respectability. He made dust into gold, and back again.

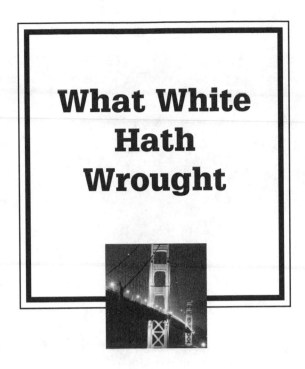

What White Hath Wrought

Only nine days after the Jonestown Massacre left 912 bodies rotting in the sun, and San Francisco rocking in the aftermath, a disgruntled ex-supervisor sneaked into City Hall carrying a loaded handgun and shot and killed Mayor George Moscone and Supervisor Harvey Milk at close range.

It was November 27, 1978, and ex-cop and recently resigned supervisor Dan White had a score to settle with both victims. Moscone had refused to give him his job back after he had a change of heart and tried to regain his seat on the Board. Milk, one of the first openly gay elected officials in America, opposed White's reinstatement. Within seconds, both were dead.

The drama that followed was beyond comprehension even to those who'd lived in San Francisco all their lives. The City had apparently taken leave of its senses. The violence portended a new and deadly era of casual killing in the nation at large. Nowadays, it seems quite common for an angry former employee to return to his workplace with a gun and murder people wantonly. But in 1978, it was an unknown custom in America. And Dan White got off with eight years on a "Twin-

Dan White (center) is led through the Hall of Justice to trial for the murder of Moscone and Milk, 1978. (*Bettmann*)

kie" defense, precipitating the White Night Riot in which protesters literally battered down the doors of City Hall.

Although White and Milk were enemies, and Dan actually killed Harvey, both were gay.

The difference was that Harvey Milk was publicly and proudly gay, while Dan White was married with children and in the closet. His homophobia amounted to self-hatred. While Dan White complained about the encroachment of aggressive homosexuals in San Francisco, he was himself sleeping with a City fireman.

Dianne Feinstein was the president of the Board of Supervisors at the time and so became mayor of San Francisco in Moscone's stead. "I always wanted to be mayor, but not this way," she said. Her political career, which had been sagging, was revived by her boss's assassination, and she went on to the U.S. Senate in 1993.

Harvey Milk might well have become mayor if he'd lived. He was an extraordinary character who parlayed a Castro Street photo store

George Moscone, 1978. (*Bettmann*)

and engaging personality into a broad base of support. He represented the most forward-looking views of the 1970s. He was against runaway expansion of San Francisco and concerned for environmental standards. He championed the rights of the poor and residents of low-income housing. And, of course, being gay, he would liberalize the City's attitudes and strip the vice squad of its powers. Some of his other ideas were entirely socialist, such as having San Francisco take over the gas and electric company.

He also predicted, more than once, that "some nut" would someday shoot him in the head for the beliefs he espoused.

His first forays into politics were disastrous. Milk couldn't even get the endorsement of the leading gay political clubs in his first run for supervisor. The gay activists considered him too erratic to make a good spokesman for their cause. Harvey was known to mouth off, lose his temper, go on a rampage. He was one of the initiators of the gay boycott against Coors Beer, whose corporate fathers made enormous contributions to right-wing homophobic causes.

The boycott actually worked, and gay power was born, tenuously, in San Francisco. An important part of Harvey's base came from the labor unions, who admired his organizing strength and ability to deliver results, overcoming their traditional loathing of fruits and queers. The Building and Construction Trades Union eventually endorsed Milk for Supe.

Dennis Peron, who in 1969 ran a marijuana store out of his Castro apartment, was one of Harvey's earliest supporters. He organized the first Harvey Milk Democratic Club (there are now many across the nation) and handed out free joints with a smile. Twenty-five years later, in 1994, Peron was still selling marijuana, but now from a

Harvey Milk, the first openly gay elected official in America, after his
1977 election to the Board of Supervisors. (*Bettmann*)

"supermarket" providing it as medical relief for AIDS and cancer
patients.

Peron was there on election night in 1975, when George Moscone,
fresh from victory in the mayoral primary, visited Harvey's defeat party
(Milk finished sixth in a field of seven) and extended his hand. Two
years later, Milk would finally become a supervisor. A year after that,
a martyr.

When he finally achieved success in 1977, Harvey was joined on
the Board of Supes by another freshman, a former policeman named
Daniel James White who seemed on the surface of things to be everything Harvey was not. He seemed as straight as an arrow, for one thing.

Still outraged: Five hundred demonstrators rally in Union Square when Dan White is released after only four years in prison, 1983. (*Bettmann*)

Conservative, Irish-Catholic, and a native San Franciscan, he deplored the immigration of "social deviates" into the old neighborhoods. In his early thirties, Dan White was relatively young for a supervisor; Harvey was fifty when Danny killed him.

Dan White was a troubled and perplexing character. Perhaps his being in the closet had much to do with it, because he was nervous, fidgety, paranoid. A great deal was expected of him, and he felt under pressure. Unlike Milk, who took every opportunity to exert his influence on the Board and the mayor, Dan White retreated into a shell. He started missing meetings. When he did show up, he sat sullenly, without making any comments. He seemed uninterested in the work of running the City. Finally, he resigned his post, stating that he couldn't support his family on the $9,600-a-year salary of a supervisor.

That was a blow to his supporters and constituents, and after a few days of listening to their encouragement, White decided to go to the mayor and ask that his resignation be withdrawn, so he could resume his position. But Mayor Moscone, almost certainly after consultation with Harvey Milk, had already decided to appoint someone else to White's seat.

Dan White fumed and talked to himself for days, then armed himself with a concealed pistol and managed to get around the metal detectors and into City Hall by climbing through a first-floor men's room window. Within minutes, the evil deeds were done and Dianne Feinstein was making her now famous speech to the hastily assembled press: "Both Mayor Moscone and Supervisor Milk have been shot and killed. The suspect is Dan White."

White walked out of City Hall unapprehended and took refuge in a Catholic church in his neighborhood before turning himself in to authorities. Instantly, his defense team began building an image of their client, who had killed two public officials in cold blood at their working desks, as himself the victim—the good boy, the good cop, the family man, driven to impassioned desperation by the machinations of liberal politics, the invasion of homosexuals in city government, and—worst of all—a junk food diet of too many hamburgers and Twinkie cakes.

The infamous Twinkie defense worked perfectly as the jury learned to feel sorry for this otherwise perfectly upright, respectable homeboy who loved San Francisco and wanted to protect it from outsiders, this cherub who slaughtered two elected officials in their course of duty. At worst, he could have been sentenced to life in state prison without parole. Instead, he got just under eight years and actually served only four. When the sentence was read, the gay community rioted like no gay crowd had rioted since Stonewall in New York in 1969. They threw rocks at police, overturned squad cars, and bashed down the glass doors of City Hall. The night after the White Night Riot, vengeful po-

Candlelight vigil for Moscone and Milk, 1978. (*Bettmann*)

licemen stormed the gay bars on Castro Street with nightsticks flailing. It was civil war. It was a travesty of justice.

On October 23, 1985, two years after his release, White committed suicide. His brother found him slumped over the steering wheel of his car, a garden hose taped from the muffler pipe into the sealed vehicle. Suicide notes and a tape of a sad Irish ballad were found nearby. The ballad ended, "Oh my God, what have they done to the town I loved so well?"

Harvey Milk's friend Dennis Peron is always running for San Francisco supervisor these days. He is more or less a perennial candidate. "Not a day goes by when I don't think of him," Peron said of Harvey. Although his career in public office was brief, and he wasn't the first openly gay elected official in the United States (that honor belongs to lesbian Elaine Noble, elected to the Massachusetts legislature in 1974), Harvey Milk was the first gay hero and martyr. The first gay and lesbian march on Washington in 1979 was held in his honor. From a small camera shop on Castro Street in San Francisco sprang a legend that grows greater every year and a movement that transforms the lives of millions.

The Disappearing Chief of Police

When Richard Hongisto was named San Francisco's chief of police in 1992, local wag Tom Rhoades said, "People are going to be walking down the street smoking a joint," just as in the Hippie era. Hongisto was famously liberal, a friend to the gay community, a swinger. He was diametrically opposite in reputation and style from his L.A. counterpart, the stern Daryl Gates. Everybody just assumed that with Dick Hongisto in charge, the City would groove.

So it came as a complete shock when, forty-five days into his term as top cop, Hongisto was fired for ordering his men to confiscate four thousand copies of a gay newspaper that lampooned him with a front-page cartoon. It didn't help Hongisto's case that he had also come down on the City with a virtual declaration of martial law in the wake of rioting after the Rodney King verdict and had imprisoned four hundred innocent bystanders for thirty-two hours in dehumanizing conditions. Among the detainees was the wife of the Associated Press Bureau chief, Judy Spratling.

The gay tabloid, the *San Francisco Bay Times*, printed a caricature of Hongisto holding a police baton between his legs under the headline "Dick's Cool New Tool: Martial Law."

Starting off on the wrong foot: Police Chief Richard Hongisto amid the Rodney King riot paraphernalia confiscated under Hongisto's policy of virtual martial law. (*AP/Wide World Photos*)

It's unclear exactly why, but the cartoon apparently drove Hongisto into a fit. In any case, he told his subordinates to remove thousands of the newspapers in clear violation of the First Amendment to the Constitution. It's really uncool, especially in San Francisco, to mess with the freedom of the press.

Yuerba Buena, Whence It Came

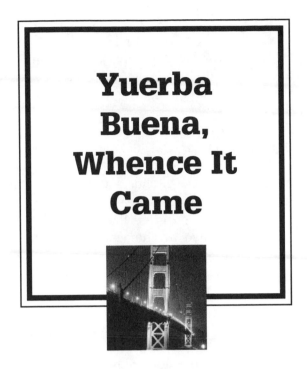

Conceding that San Francisco is the American city most associated with pot and other drug use, you have to remember that rural areas of California directly to its north are famous for cultivating the strongest grass in the nation. Only Hawaiian stuff can compete with the heady sinsemilla of the Emerald Triangle—the counties of Mendocino, Trinity, and Humboldt. What grows in "them thar hills" winds up for sale on the slopes of San Francisco.

And, from all appearances, bumper crops are in the future. During the strongly prohibitive Reagan years, the so-called war on drugs funded a paramilitary effort to eradicate pot growing in northern California, but everyone now agrees the pot growers won the battle.

The Campaign Against Marijuana Planting (or CAMP) at one time enjoyed the largesse of a $3 million annual budget. It was down to $800,000 in 1994. The National Guard will no longer lend its helicopters to this Vietnam-style terrorism of overhead surveillance and swooping raids by camouflage-clad warriors. Only one lone employee remains on the payroll of what was once a huge federal boondoggle.

The Clinton administration has opted for more treatment and prevention of addiction, fewer kamikaze attacks and seizures. All of San Francisco's many potheads are rejoicing at this news, as it seems certain to bring more grass into the market, reducing the price as availability soars.

One sheriff's deputy predicted a "glut on the market," which will be "reflected in lower prices." But Allen St. Pierre, president of the National Organization for the Reform of Marijuana Laws (NORML), countered that CAMP was being shut down because "officials are heeding the public's cries about overzealous eradicators."

Indeed, CAMP guerrillas terrorized the innocent along with the guilty for ten years. People had their homes taken away for the heinous crime of growing five or six plants. Children were traumatized by the constant presence of helicopters and military assaults. The noise, gunfire, and mayhem greatly disturbed the otherwise sleepy composure of these far-flung outposts.

All of this was in a losing cause. Even the most aggressively pro-CAMP commandos admitted that 80 percent of the pot growth north of San Francisco escaped detection. In the 1980s, new strains of pot were developed that mature faster and are more difficult to spot from aerial surveillance. Indoor cultivation has become more popular, too. With diminished funds and manpower, CAMP can't hope to block the shipment of more than a token amount of pot into San Francisco.

The '90s are making like the '60s in Baghdad by the Bay. Brother, can you spare a joint?

Be Sure to Wear a Flower in Your Hair

While the war in Vietnam consumed the late 1960s in its fiery wake, and students in Berkeley fomented campus insurrection, the formerly quiet intersection of Haight and Ashbury in San Francisco became synonymous with the ultimate symbol of rebellion, the Hippie.

The Hippie was some kind of evolution of the Beatnik but carried the movement higher. While Beatniks may have smoked pot, Hippies tripped on acid. San Francisco Hippies in particular, insistently unled by nonleaders, publicizing themselves in a colorful "underground" newspaper called the *Oracle*, caught the attention of the world.

They were smelly and strange, mostly white, middle-class young people who had willingly thrown off all their parents' materialistic security. They lived together in heaps (called communes), took over the funky Victorian boarding houses of the Haight neighborhood, grew long hair and beards, scorned work and responsibility, and professed a New Age based on love and cosmic peace. They weren't political like the student demonstrators of the New Left; they were in fact apolitical, dropouts from the American dream. They asked only to be left alone to chant mantras, experiment with free sex, and forge a new world based on good vibrations and brotherhood.

Dr. Timothy Leary, poet Allen Ginsberg, and the raffish Abbie Hoffman were all considerably older than the average Hippie in the Haight, but they were seen as leaders. Ginsberg is credited as the organizer of the phenomenal "Human Be-In" in Golden Gate Park during the celestial Summer of Love, 1967. Any disaffected kid in America who was sick of his or her parents, loved rock and roll, and could hitchhike out to San Francisco was there. There were no speeches, democratic voting, or Hippie platforms extolled. Just a sea of stoned-to-the-gills Hippies grooving on each other in the golden sunshine of San Francisco. *Life* magazine featured color photo coverage. Fifteen-year-olds in Ohio and New Jersey and South Dakota simply packed their bags and left home.

The Hippies were everywhere by 1970, yet they were always associated with San Francisco—they "came from" there. It was easier, certainly, to live on scant resources in San Francisco than in, say, New York, with its colder weather and tougher attitude. Frisco was Open, was Cool. (In more ways than one. Often, the flower children from the East found that while "it never rains in southern California," it's often freezing in the San Francisco fog of July and August.)

Hippie music was amply provided by Janis Joplin, Big Brother and the Holding Company, Country Joe and the Fish, and the Grateful Dead—all California traditions—and LSD was served free in a spiked punch at many of the concerts. It was never a hassle to get high. You could walk through the Haight and be invited to share joints with total strangers.

There was for a brief few years a feeling of absolute freedom in the Hippie experiment. People actually believed they could live for free, without working at a job, sharing with their fellow humans, loving openly. Sexual lumpings, group humpings were commonplace. The Hippie vocabulary relied heavily on *man* and *far out*. Anarchy reigned in many of the communes and underground freak "organizations," so that any adolescent who arrived yesterday could declare himself or herself a member of the "entire staff" and "family."

The dark side of all this was hideous. Charles Manson and his murder squad were Hippies gone bad. Haight Ashbury became overrun with heroin and cocaine dealers and petty criminals by the early 1970s,

We got the funk: Far-out outfits prevail in the hippie utopia that was San Francisco of 1967. (*Bettman*)

The Grateful Dead—the early years. (*Bettman*)

Janis Joplin with flowers in her hair and nothing left to lose, Golden Gate Park, 1968. (*Bettmann*)

a bombed-out urban nightmare and no vision of Hippie Utopia. The true Hippies always blamed the media for destroying the place by sensationally reporting on it around the world, but you couldn't really blame the press for picking up on a newsworthy phenomenon: the spectacle of American kids turning against their parents' mores, making San Francisco into a new lost world.

The Summer of Love, 1967

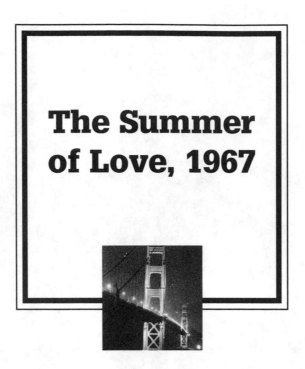

"It was the San Francisco Be-In, the Gathering of the Tribes that January [1967] in Golden Gate Park, that changed the way we looked at ourselves. Before, there seemed to be about twenty of us, our friends and their friends. Suddenly there were thousands of people, and we felt this tremendous strength in numbers. No one was trying to do any damage to anyone else, and there was a real sense that we all coexisted in as near perfect harmony as human beings are capable of."

—PAUL KANTNER,
Member of the Jefferson Airplane

"When I see friends from that time, well, we're like soldiers who were in a really successful campaign. We wear these invisible ribbons, and we always grin when we see them on each other. Have I given up on the spirit of that time? Ya never quits da mob."

—KEN KESEY,
of the Merry Pranksters

The Summer of Love, 1967

"One reason for the decline of that era . . . was the advent of professional dealers. In a very few months, around the end of 1967, it went from disorganized crime to highly organized crime. . . . Suddenly things got ugly."

—STEWART BRAND,
publisher of the **Whole Earth Catalog**

"I always think of it in light of Paris in the '20s, a kind of mini-Renaissance. The culture was repressed, and that repression, I think, resulted in a flowering of the avant-garde."

—GEORGE HUNTER,
Concert promoter

"Could it happen again? I'm sure it will. . . . But I'm not sure it will ever match the breadth and strength of the Hippies. That was truly an extraordinary experiment in living."

—TERENCE HALLINAN,
San Francisco attorney

This Is
Berkeley,
Baby

Some things never change. The '60s are long gone, but in Berkeley, just over the Bay Bridge from the City, there is still a grungy plot of land called People's Park, owned by the University of California and never developed because of fear of popular wrath. People's Park was the 1969 battleground between Governor Ronald Reagan, two thousand National Guard troops, and a citizenry as radical and far out as any in the world.

Hundreds were arrested, scores wounded, and one man was killed in the battle for People's Park. Today, the issue is not whether the park can survive, but whether the volleyball courts there are detrimental to the rights of the homeless who sleep in the park. Berkeley is the only city in America with an all-homeless basketball team (they play against college teams) and a special fund for the pets of the homeless.

The once famous Berkeley Food Co-Op in 1991 became the Whole Foods Market, a mecca for those who prefer tofu to boogie meat, but controversy erupted over Whole Foods' adamant stance against unions. While union pickets marched outside, slightly embarrassed New Agers crossed the line to get their sprouts.

People's Park, Berkeley's shrine to the sixties, 1989.
(*AP/Wide World Photos*)

A *Playboy* magazine read-in at Berkeley? Yes, it happened in 1992 after a waitress at Bette's Ocean View Diner objected to a male customer who was reading *Playboy* at his table and asked him to ditch the mag or move to a more obscure corner of the restaurant.

Straight (one may assume) males led the read-in, which featured guys reading *Playboy* over their hot dogs and chili. Feminists protested by wearing penis-shaped nose appendages and declaring the guys to be "dickheads."

A spokesman for the read-inners said, "No one appoints waitresses or other customers as a judge or jury of our reading." The women screamed, "You fucking hypocrite, take off your clothes. We want to measure your dick."

In Berkeley, the value of the average trashed-looking stucco cottage peaked at about a half million dollars in the early 1990s. You might be able to afford to rent, but you can no longer buy a house there unless you're relatively rich by American middle-class standards.

Pass the (Wavy) Gravy

Wavy Gravy, as everyone knows him, was born Hugh Romney and first achieved renown as the most publicized member of the Hog Farm semi-political, semi-Hippie commune north of the City. He was also the "please chief" of the Woodstock Nation, using seltzer bottles and cream pies as his weapons to keep order at that 1969 gathering. He uses humor to put across his political philosophy of peace and love, and for a change this politician really is funny.

Wavy invented the Nobody for President campaign in 1976. "From 1976 to the present, I've continued to work for Nobody 'cuz Nobody is in Washington working for me," he once wrote.

Among other things, Wavy Gravy is the director of Camp Winna-rainbow, a circus and performing arts summer camp in the north woods near Laytonville, and it was there that he received the call in 1990. A left-wing group called Berkeley Citizens Action asked him to run for the Berkeley city council against a powerful conservative (for Berkeley) incumbent, Shirley Dean. "Tell them I'll do it if I can run as a clown," he replied. Wavy's been going around dressed as a clown since that fateful day at a demonstration at People's Park in Berkeley

Wavy Gravy campaigns for Nobody. (*Lisa Law*)

when he discovered that "the police did not want to hit me any more. Clowns are safe."

Once he'd decided to take up the political challenge, Wavy had to deal with the city clerk, who wanted to know whether he would be listed on the ballot as (1) Hugh Romney, (2) Hugh Romney a.k.a. Wavy Gravy, (3) Hugh "Wavy Gravy" Romney, or (4) just plain Wavy Gravy. He chose the last, or course. Who ever heard of Hugh Romney, anyway? His campaign committee then started passing out red rubber noses in exchange for contributions and printed a colorful flyer reading, "Lets Elect a Real Clown for a Change."

The media came to attention. ABC News ran a feature. Jane Gross interviewed Wavy for the *New York Times*. Congressman Ron Dellums, who became chair of the House Armed Services Committee in Clinton's administration, endorsed the zany Gravy—got on the Gravy Train, so to speak. Other endorsements came from Ram Dass, the New Age guru, and Rusty Schweickart, the astronaut. ("From innerspace to outer space," Wavy quipped.) The *Economist* and the *Observer* from England wrote about Wavy's campaign, and radio interviewers called from as far afield as Nebraska and Berlin.

The press really had a field day when Ken Kesey got into the act, resurrecting his old psychedelic bus, Further, for "a historical reunion." Down the main boulevards of Berkeley they rode, Merry Pranksters and all, to the blazing soundtrack of "Hit the Road, Jack." Up into the Berkeley hills they ground, determined to put acid into the city water supply. The caravan got seven minutes' coverage on CNN News.

Worthy opponent Shirley Dean finally agreed to debate Wavy on KPFA radio, the FM equivalent of the Communist party's old *Daily Worker*. Serious and sober as usual, she railed on about the problems Berkeley has with speeders, sewers, and potholes. ("She said she wanted to *fix* Berkeley, as if the city were a giant cat," Wavy laughed.) Wavy countered that she should think of the potholes as "reverse

Ken Kesey takes a last trip on his psychedelic bus, revived here for its delivery to the Smithsonian Institution. (*AP/Wide World Photos*)

speed bumps" and that Berkeley should spend more on its homeless and its youth. "I've got it," he said, "we need a chicken in every pothole. No, make that a *rubber* chicken in every pothole (not to offend animal rights advocates)."

In the end, of course, Shirley Dean won the city council seat, with four thousand votes to Wavy's two thousand. "Such a relief!" quoth the clown. "Sure, I could have done it different . . . put my clown suit in the closet and dressed up in straight clothing. . . . What we did was tickle the political fancy of a nation bored shitless with the usual bill of fare." A TV commentator in the Soviet Union reported that "a just and serious clown" was running for office in California, the state that gave us a B-movie actor for president, a tap dancer for congressman, and Sonny Bono for mayor of Palm Springs.

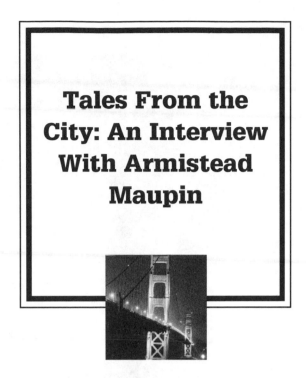

Tales From the City: An Interview With Armistead Maupin

With the 1994 PBS broadcast of his "Tales of the City" miniseries (produced in England by the BBC), Armistead Maupin made the leap from San Francisco celebrity and popular novelist to world-renowned literary light. The tales depict San Francisco in the 1970s, a fictional pastiche based closely on social reality. Some of the characters, like Maupin himself, are gay, and many of them freely use pot and cocaine. Frank, matter-of-fact images of homosexuality and recreational drug use became the boldest ever seen on national TV.

This interview with Armistead Maupin was taped in San Francisco as his novel *Significant Others*, part of the Tales of the City series, was about to be published. He and his lover, Terry Anderson, joked and bantered about the issues of the day. Terry is HIV-positive and has suffered occasional health concerns, while Armistead is HIV-negative and one of the first to publicly preach safe sex and the safety of intimacy with the HIV-positive.

From the tape:

Our interview with Armistead Maupin, acclaimed author of *Tales of the City*, *Babycakes*, and the new *Significant Others*, took place in his beloved San Francisco on a balmy Mother's Day Sunday. Terry Anderson, Armistead's own "significant other," joined me in a stroll through the Noe Valley from the author's warmly colorful apartment, with views of City hills, down to Leticia's restaurant, a short block from the Walt Whitman Bookshop in the Castro District, where *Significant Others* held court in the window display.

The arrival of Maupin in the restaurant caused an immediate stir, with Sunday brunch patrons straining eagerly for a glimpse of one of San Francisco's most admired writers.

Armistead Maupin, 1992. (*Robert Foothorap, courtesy of HarperCollins*)

RM: Tell us about *Significant Others*. It's from Harper and Row, and what's the pub date?

ARMISTEAD MAUPIN: June 3, but it's already out.

WAITER: Will you gentlemen have anything to drink this morning?

RM: I'll have a Bloody Mary.

AM: I'll have the same, actually. No, make that a Margarita.

WAITER: Large or small?

AM: Large.

RM: Do you do any promoting before June 3?

AM: It really means the publicity starts in New York on June 3. The book is out, and I'm doing publicity here.

RM: But you are going to do a tour, right?

AM: Ten cities, fourteen days.

RM: Terry, are you going with him?

TERRY ANDERSON: On half of it. I'm going to stop in Atlanta and spend some days there.

An Interview With Armistead Maupin

RM: Are you doing any national shows?

AM: I'm told there's a possibility of "The Today Show," but it hasn't been decided yet. Jane Pauley apparently gets most of the queers. (*Laughter.*)

RM: You would do well on "The Today Show."

AM: I'm not planning on it. I really don't know what other ones they've got lined up. I'm like an actor with his audience; you really get to find out how people are reacting to the book.

RM: Well, the feedback from the announcement that you and Tom Robbins will appear together at the Writers' Jamboree in Carmel has been wonderful. People are excited about it. You and Robbins both have cult followings.

(*A toast is raised; congratulations and much success.*)

AM: The trick is to stay fresh on the tour. When *Babycakes* came out in 1984, it was the first time Harper and Row sent me on an extensive tour. They said, "Are you sure you want to do this? A lot of authors don't like to do it," and I said, "But of course I want to do it, this is what I've spent my life trying to make happen." Then about six days into the tour, I heard myself answer the same four questions over and over again and began to get a little disgusted at the sound of my own voice.

RM: It's any good actor's job to make it seem really original even if they've said it a million times before.

AM: Exactly. And you're asked the same four questions because they are the four questions that should be asked.

RM: Does Harper and Row take decent care of you on the road? Do they put you in good hotels?

AM: Yes, they did last time around, and I expect they will again. I got lots of complimentary soaps and shampoos.

RM: Wonderful! It matters so much that you can get good rest.

AM: Especially since I spend all of my time in my hotel room when I'm not promoting. There are people who say, "We want to show you the sights," but I'm in a work mode and not able to break out of it.

RM: Do you watch TV?

AM: I watch TV. I love "Three's Company." That's the darkest secret I have. There's something so mindless about "Three's Company," I find it comforting. I don't know what it is. Most bad TV I can't tolerate.

RM: Terry, you're editing the program for the annual Gay Pride Parade, but you say you're not really an editor.

TA: I'm more of an organizer. That's how I met Armistead in Atlanta.

WAITER: Are you guys ready to order?

RM: I'll have the eggs Benedict with the shrimp.

WAITER: Benny Shrimp?

AM: That's a shrimp on speed.

TA: Two.

AM: I'll have the regular eggs Benedict. This restaurant used to have a transsexual hostess, very beautiful and quite charming. I brought my father here one night with my stepmother, who's a year younger than I am, and my father spent the whole evening flirting with the hostess. At one point he asked her if there were any more like her back home in South Carolina.

RM: Was he aware of her . . . uh . . .?

AM: I told him after that remark, and curiously he became even more fascinated. He started grabbing her waist and saying, "What a nice firm waist she's got, honey," making my stepmother wildly jealous.

RM: How old is your father?

AM: Seventy-four at this point.

RM: Does he approve of your lifestyle?

AM: We have a kind of understanding, yes. He sasses me and I sass him.

RM: But you're open about it.

AM: He's always been a Rabelaisian sort of person, and he just applied it to my life. He's deeply enmeshed with Jerry Falwell and those types.

RM: Don't you just love the tale of the destruction of the PTL empire?

AM: Yes, it's so satisfying to watch the news.

RM: What do you think about the "Jim Bakker is a homosexual" allegations?

AM: How could any self-respecting homosexual allow his wife to do her eyes like that?

RM: Did you happen to see in the *Chronicle* "How to Make Your Face Up Like Tammy Faye Bakker?"

AM: Take two charcoal briquettes . . .

TA: PTL stands for "Pay for Tammy's Lashes."

An Interview With Armistead Maupin

RM: Between Irangate and the Jim and Tammy thing, the news has been so amusing lately.

TA: And the press is trying to get Gary Hart because he had sex with someone.

RM: The press doesn't like Gary Hart.

AM: Four years ago they tried to get him by describing the quiche lunch he had with Jerry Brown. They had a powwow in Big Sur, and the press called it a "quiche lunch." What could be more damning?

RM: Especially with Jerry Brown. Thank God we don't have any quiche here. But you write so well about gays, you must be very well adjusted.

AM: I'm thoroughly convinced that the responsibility lies with gay people to be open about who they are. We cannot expect the world to accept and understand us if we don't communicate.

TA: And gay or straight, there are a lot of people who are fucked up about their lives. It has nothing to do with their sexuality.

AM: One of the reasons I'm excited about meeting Tom Robbins is that he's a guy who is obviously joyfully comfortable with his sexuality.

RM: We've never had a bad time with the dude, and we hung out for many years.

AM: "The dude." You'll never call me a dude.

WAITER: Benny shrimp, Benny shrimp, Benny.

TA: I think the world is divided into two segments, people who like sex and those who don't. Sex is a liberator, it really is.

AM: Our worst presidents have been the ones who had no sex lives.

RM: Jimmy Carter was supposedly the only one who actually slept with his wife.

AM: Well, Mamie Eisenhower apparently insisted on sleeping with Ike.

RM: This is probably the one question everybody asks you, but how do you feel about the *Examiner* vis-à-vis the *Chronicle*? You wrote *Tales of the City* for the *Chron* but switched to the *Examiner* for *Significant Others*. In the past year, the *Examiner* has taken on a number of good writers.

AM: The *Chronicle* was indifferent to my offer. I wasn't trying to hold them up for a lot of money. In fact, we hadn't even discussed money. They were resisting dealing with my agent. They put me in a reporter status after ten years of my bringing them a great deal of income. They own 30 percent of my first four books.

RM: It seems rather foolish of them to let you go. You're one of their most popular writers.

AM: They're arrogant. They're the only game in town in their own eyes. What they miscalculated on is my need for a large daily circulation. I'm essentially writing for the book form now. I don't really care where it appears in newspaper form. I do give the *Chronicle* credit for endorsing a fairly controversial concept. *Tales of the City* was after all the first serial fiction to appear in an American daily for something like thirty years.

RM: You revived an old form very successfully.

AM: But I didn't know I had a book at the time. I had a better deal than most columnists; the others had to give up 50 percent of their income to the *Chronicle* for any outside exploitation of the work. They gave me a better deal only because they figured it wouldn't "play" outside the Bay Area. I recently ran into the editor of Chronicle Books and teased him about passing me up, and he said, "Oh, we can top that. We turned down Gary Larson." Frankly, no one was more surprised than I was when Harper and Row came to me with an offer.

RM: But you achieved a nationwide readership.

AM: Actually an international one. It's been translated into Dutch, German, Spanish, and there's also a British edition.

TA: One of the Tales books was seized by Customs entering South Africa.

RM: Too heavy for South Africa!

AM: It was seized by Customs in England for being lewd and lascivious. They look for gay- and lesbian-type matter, and if they find it, they automatically assume it's lewd and lascivious.

RM: But there are no graphic sex scenes whatsoever.

AM: The new one has more than the earlier ones.

RM: Tell us about it. Is there a character in it who has AIDS, or is that a mystery we have to read the book to find out?

AM: Yes, there's a heterosexual character who may have AIDS. One of my editors at Harper and Row said he was amazed that I was able to write a novel that's so on top of the times. "You have a novel about heterosexual AIDS just as it's being discussed." I said, "What do you mean, just as it's being discussed? We've been dealing with this for over five years!"

RM: Maybe New York is behind the times.

WAITER: Would you like another drink, gentlemen?

RM: White wine.

AM: White wine.

WAITER: Let me bring you half a carafe, same price and you'll get a little more wine.

RM: In New York, they hate to think they're five minutes behind us in any way, but in the area of AIDS education . . .

TA: Part of the problem in New York is they have a gay mayor, and he's afraid of any discussion of AIDS might implicate him.

RM: Ed Koch, gay? This is news.

TA: It's not news in New York.

AM: I can't do *anything* with him, he just says these things.

RM: For ten or fifteen years, I've been hanging out in New York in an apartment on the corner of Christopher and Bleecker, and I never heard anyone say Ed Koch was gay.

AM: One of the premises in Larry Kramer's *The Normal Heart* is that Koch held back on doing anything about the AIDS crisis because he was afraid people would perceive him as gay.

RM: One more song of the Closet Case Blues.

AM: I don't care how he's perceived, I'm just worried about people dying.

RM: We expect your appearance in Monterey to have a great effect on the public consciousness.

AM: I expect to have a major impact on Kim Novak's life. [Note: Novak is a Monterey Peninsula resident.] For years when I was a teenager, I told myself that I wasn't gay because, after all, I *did* like Kim Novak!

RM: *Publishers Weekly* mentioned that you became a spokesman for Rock Hudson after he was diagnosed with AIDS. Is that true?

AM: I was quoted on him. He thought his world was going to come to an abrupt and terrible end when he made that announcement [that he had AIDS]. The biggest shock was the fact that thirty thousand people wrote and said, "We love you just the way you are." It was the biggest revelation of his life, really.

RM: Then there's Liberace, who never . . .

AM: Who never felt the joy of knowing that people knew and didn't care. The sadness of that is that he was a deeply homophobic man. Rock, for all his secrecy, was not homophobic. He saw nothing wrong with the way he was. And when he realized that he was going to die and therefore no longer had a career, he said "Fuck it, we'll tell the truth." And he hired a woman to do just that.

RM: Sara Davidson? [Hudson's official biographer.]

AM: Yeah. He gave her a list of his friends to interview. She was just the right person for the job. His friend George Nader, who was the recipient of his estate, turned over his diary to Sara. She called me with some very specific questions. I had to make sure it was really Sara Davidson, because I was afraid it might be the *National Enquirer* or somebody else. People who are gay and happy being gay have to speak up, otherwise homosexuality will always be reported by the scandalmongers. We'll always be the fodder for the *National Enquirer* until we learn to be so forthright that the onus is gone.

RM: Don't you think your audience is a straight one? That is, you cut across the gay and straight line.

AM: Yes, and there's still a tendency for journalists to eliminate any mention of my homosexuality in any discussion of my work. A recent piece in *Vanity Fair* didn't mention it at all.

RM: You're a gay San Francisco writer whose audience is universal. And your characters say such funny things and think so real-ly.

AM: I think it's a function of what you tend to store. I can't remember dates or where I was or who I went to the movies with, but I will store away the line "Oh no, the vinaigrette leaked" from a camping trip to Death Valley and use it in *Babycakes*.

Sister Act

One of the more striking images in Armistead Maupin's PBS movie, "Tales of the City," which drew the wrath of Senator Jesse Helms, was that of a male "nun" skating through the Castro. The reference, no doubt, was to the Sisters of Perpetual Indulgence, gay men dressed in nun drag who recently celebrated their fifteenth anniversary in the City with an Easter Sunday "Indulgence in the Park."

These sisters, when they are not perpetually indulging themselves, also do good work for many AIDS charities in the Bay Area, according to Sister Dana Van Iquity.

The Easter Indulgence started with a High Mass at noon in the Castro's Collingwood Park and ended at nightfall as Mr. and Ms. Gay San Francisco, Jacques and Jealousy, stripped down and carried crosses. Hmmm, well, even Jesse Helms might admit that being gay and Christian at the same time is a cross to bear.

The ceremonies were presided over by Their Imperial Majesties Empress Anita Martini and Emperor Chuck Adkins. Five virgin novices of the order were invested into the Convent of Our Lady of Nuts and Bolts: Sisters Gladass of the Joyous Resserectum, Pigmential Stigmata,

Dyke Van Dick, Hellen Wheels, and Nada Christina Virgina all took their wedding vows to Christ in white gowns and wigs, then were stripped, whipped with riding crops, and finally dressed in their habits. Some habits.

This formal investiture was followed by awards. Sister Lily White Posterior Superior got the Saint Puce medallion for having been the most indulgent of all the Sisters of Perpetual Indulgence. Civic leadership awards were given to Tom Hanks (who didn't show up to collect his), Armistead Maupin, Rita Rocket, and Holly Johnson. The president of the San Francisco school board, Tom Ammiano, did show up and presented a prize to Peter Martin in the Stonewall 25 raffle.

The annual Easter bonnet contest top prizes went to chickens— well, birds. One hat featured a dead chicken, the second a live chicken, and the third a phony flamingo.

Easter was never like this in, say, Kansas.

The Real
Royalty

It's a funny thing: when people think of San Francisco's leaders, celebrities, and "famous names," they almost never think of Phil Burton and his brothers John and Bob, but you could argue that the Burtons came as close to genuine San Francisco aristocracy as anyone. No other single person had the impact on the City that Phil Burton did, yet to outsiders his name is unknown. Tony Bennett gets greater recognition for singing "I Left My Heart in San Francisco" than Phil Burton does for practically re-inventing the place.

From 1963 to 1983, Phil represented the City in the House of Representatives in Washington, after having effectively carved out his own district and then created a new one for his brother John. In 1977, Phil came within a single vote of being elected the Democratic majority leader of the House. He chaired powerful committees and pushed people around. He was a hard-drinking, driven, obsessive, ultimately brilliant politician, and when he died just like that of a burst artery, his funeral was conducted with a pomp and circumstance reserved for heads of state.

The Burton machine, as it was called, created such politicians as

Phil Burton (center) witnesses the swearing-in of his brother John
(right), 1974. (*Bettmann*)

Willie Brown, George Moscone, Art Agnos, Nancy Pelosi, and Barbara
Boxer. These are all liberals, but the Burtons were far left of center,
actual populist radicals. "I trust visceral reactions and I trust workers'
reactions," Phil once said. "I like people whose balls roar when they
see injustice!"

He started out in 1954, representing his district of San Francisco in
the California House in Sacramento. Even then, Phil had acquired a
reputation as a prodigious drinker, someone who could drink other
people under the table and seem unaffected. The first vodka on the
rocks was poured in his office in the late afternoon, and he might have
eight or ten tumblers full before dinner. He drank vodka like it was
water. Just before digging into a steak or prime rib dinner, he would
quickly down a tall glass of cold milk for the digestion, then continue
drinking vodka through the meal and into the evening. He also
smoked three packs of unfiltered cigarettes a day and was only fifty-

seven when he died, a man who abused his own body as fiercely as he championed the health of others'.

Early on, Phil had learned the art of packaging legislation with clauses and subclauses that allowed him to push through the ultra-liberal provisions so dear to his heart. He is credited with slipping California's medical welfare policy (Medi-Cal), the most inclusive in the nation, past powerful House Speaker Jesse Unruh. "No one knows what we've done here today," Phil said at the time. "This is going to cost more money than anyone can ever imagine."

If today AIDS patients flock to San Francisco, and sickly Mexicans will do anything to get across the border into San Diego, it's partly Burton's legacy. "Phil Burton was the greatest man in the history of San Francisco. He nurtured Willie, John, George, and all of those fuck-ing liberals," his brother Bob said.

Some of his proposals were too liberal even for the liberals. He once backed a plan that would have imposed a limit of $2.5 million on the personal wealth of any Californian, with the state seizing the $10 billion in excess wealth held by California's four thousand millionaires to be distributed to the poor.

Brother Johnny, the youngest of the three Burtons, was elected to the state assembly despite some run-ins with the law—public drinking and pot smoking, and one arrest for taking bets. Then-governor Ronald Reagan called him "a nut," so John fed the squirrels in the park in Sacramento for the benefit of the press. When he tried to ban the sale of toy guns in California, he brought a toy machine gun into the as-sembly chambers and pretended to shoot his fellow representatives. John never had the cunning or the temper of his older brother, though.

In 1973, Phil personally reapportioned parts of Marin County and northwest San Francisco to create a new legislative district for his kid brother John, and the Burtons became a brother act in the U.S. Con-gress. John's district was a classic gerrymander, snaking through heav-ily Democratic neighborhoods over four counties. Phil once called it "my contribution to modern art."

But as in Sacramento, John in Washington didn't have the drive or ruthlessness that Phil possessed. He didn't rise to any high committee chairmanships but was content to lobby for free toilets in government buildings and the establishment of National Grandparents' Day. After several of his marriages broke up and his best friend George Moscone was murdered in City Hall, John seemed to flip out altogether, appearing in public while evidently stoned, admitting to marijuana indulgence amid accusations of harder drug use, and giving a speech in the House of Representatives entirely in hand signals nobody could understand. Even the Burtons' mother was quoted as saying John should straighten up and fly right or at least stop flying in public.

John quit politics, declining to run again for his seat in Congress, which was taken by a young Marin County supervisor with ambitions, Barbara Boxer. She's now in the U.S. Senate.

Phil just went on terrorizing Washington, drinking and getting fat, but handily winning re-election by huge margins. He was virtually "Mr. San Francisco" in the federal government structure. But his body couldn't hold out, and he died suddenly in a suite at the Saint Francis Hotel in 1983. His body lay in state in the grand rotunda of San Francisco City Hall while thousands filed past. A large contingent from Congress, headed by Phil's cagy enemy Tip O'Neill, came to San Francisco for a huge, glorious funeral service in Gold Gate National Recreation Area, a national park that was one of Phil's proudest creations for his hometown constituency.

Phil's wife, Sala, announced her candidacy for his seat in Congress within days of his death and was elected in a breeze, then re-elected twice more before she also died in her third term.

Johnny eventually returned to the state assembly, but the years of Burton hegemony in Washington were over and never returned. While Phil was in Congress, blustering everyone in sight, San Francisco remained the political center of the state of California, the power base, notwithstanding Los Angeles' growing edge in population and money.

Since he died and his wife also passed away, there has been no one from San Francisco wielding the kind of power in Washington that Phil Burton had, and people say the City has faded to an anachronism, a pale shadow of its former self, an old dowager living on its memories of former grandeur. L.A. has the clout, Phil Burton is gone, and who remembers?

Another Kind of Church

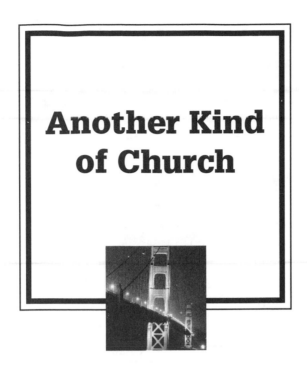

The Church of the Secret Gospel at 744–46 Clementina St. in the South of Market District dispensed more than holy water. Beer, for one thing. Unsafe sex, for another. Operating under the guise of a religion, the church was an underground sex club featuring "glory holes"— holes cut into walls to facilitate oral sex—dark, dark orgy areas.

High priests "Father" Frank and "Reverend" Donald Jackson were prohibited from advertising the club, which was closed by the City's health department on December 22, 1993, for "contributing to the spread of the AIDS virus." The order from county health officer Sandra Hernandez, M.D., noted that San Francisco has the highest per capita rate of AIDS infection in the entire United States and condemned the church for refusing to comply with safe sex guidelines.

This particular religion didn't go in for candlelight, or much other light either, and San Francisco now requires that its sex clubs be well enough lit that sexual activity can be "monitored," for the benefit of the participants, not just the voyeurs.

AIDS Office director Dr. Mitch Katz did concede that the church could reopen its doors with the city attorney's consent if it cleaned up its act.

The Church of the Secret Gospel was one of four such sex clubs cited and closed in late 1993, proving that San Francisco continues to find ways to reinvent the 1970s bathhouse/orgy club environment for which the City became famous. As for the risk of HIV infection and subsequent death, some gay men in San Francisco have simply become resigned to its "inevitability."

This attitude has health officials worried about a potential second wave of AIDS in the city. Surveys from the Center for AIDS Prevention at the University of California at San Francisco show rising rates of both infection and unsafe behavior. Among every hundred uninfected gay men in San Francisco in 1993, four men under twenty-five years old got infected. Two men over that age. That's double to quadruple the 1985 rate of one man per hundred. (But still much lower than the staggering rate of eighteen per hundred back in 1982.)

The problem is not education but emotions. San Franciscans are probably better educated about the causes of AIDS than any other Americans. "Everybody" knows that anal intercourse without a condom is the most risky kind of sex, and it's believed that fully half the gay male population in San Francisco carries the HIV virus.

But there are still emotions to contend with, much the same kind of emotions that compel people to jump off the Golden Gate Bridge. Guys just give up rather than face the daunting prospect of a lifetime denial of intimacy and sexual excitement. Safe sex is boring, some believe. Others envy the attention and love showered on those who are dying of AIDS. The very young guys still have that young-guy attitude of invulnerability, while the middle-aged and older guys think that with luck one can survive having HIV a good ten years or more, so they won't die that much younger than normal anyway. There's a disturbing pattern of surrender.

Bill Graham,
San Francisco's
Rock
Impresario

Born Wolfgang Grajonca in Berlin in 1931, he didn't know his parents, escaped the Nazis by walking across Europe to eventual freedom in France, and arrived in New York as an orphaned teenager. Wolfgang became William, Grajonca became Graham, and Bill Graham became the greatest entrepreneur in rock and roll concert history. He made San Francisco the world capital of his own business and of rock music.

After the terrible experience of rejection by many prospective foster parents, Graham was taken in by the Alfred Ehrenrich family in the Bronx, and eventually he was reunited with his sisters. But his traumatized childhood and consequent insecurity led to the development of a businessman who was criticized for being greedy, bossy, and megalomaniacal. Bill Graham had to be in control. Even when his enterprises had reached multimillion-dollar levels, he personally supervised the cash register receipts because he didn't trust anyone else to do it.

Drafted to serve in the army during the Korean War, Bill had his first exposure to San Francisco while shipping out to the Far East. Like so

Legendary rock impressario Bill Graham (center) hosts a fundraiser with Mayor Alioto (left) and Willie Mays (right), 1975. (*Bettmann*)

many others, he fell in love with the City and, after his military service ended, began living there. His first digs were a rundown boarding house at 323 Locust Street, but he would go on to taste the fruits of the high lifestyle in Baghdad by the Bay.

Bill's first theatrical experience in the City was with the nascent San Francisco Mime Troupe in the early 1960s. The now famous Mime Troupe was not limited to mime, or silent, performances. They also did plays and revues, mostly of a political and satirical bent. Bill was one of their first active participants, along with Ronny Davis, the founder, but eventually the two broke up in quarrels and rivalry.

It was the Mime Troupe's first successful benefit that laid the groundwork for what would become Bill Graham's career as a concert producer and event organizer. The Troupe had been busted by the San Francisco police for performing without a permit in Golden Gate Park. Bill masterminded a benefit performance program to raise money for the group's legal fees, and in one exhilarating night at an overcrowded loft, the Mime Troupe pocketed $4,200. Specifically, Bill Graham pocketed the money, taking it home with him in his knapsack for safekeeping. From that point on, he said, he realized he "had the knack" for organizing musical events, a polite term for what often turned out to be public riots.

After leaving the Mime Troupe, Bill opened the original Fillmore Auditorium on the corner of Fillmore and Geary, resurrecting one of San Francisco's old, downtrodden vaudeville halls. His first big event was the Trips Festival, a psychedelic, LSD-dripping, mind-blowing public orgy of rock music and acid sponsored by the likes of Ken Kesey, the Merry Pranksters, Ramon Sender, and Stewart Brand of the *Whole Earth Catalog*, another uniquely San Franciscan institution. Music was headlined by Big Brother and the Holding Company. Acid by Owsley was in the punch.

Bill objected to the free distribution of world-class-strength LSD at these concerts. Just as any other businessperson might, he worried that people might get hurt, especially if they didn't know what they were imbibing or had no experience with acid. There was the question of legal liability. And Graham, although known to take drugs himself, was no Hippie. He was a Holocaust survivor making a good living on the Hippie subculture in San Francisco.

After the Trips Festival, Jefferson Airplane became the big attraction at the Fillmore. Then came the Grateful Dead and Paul Butterfield Blues Band, great acts promoted by a great huckster. Graham hit the streets of the City with his roughly printed posters of bleeding color and twisted lettering. Janis Joplin, Chuck Berry, B. B. King, Otis Redding, Eric Clapton, Muddy Waters, the Byrds, the Who—the list of artists who played the Fillmore is endless. All the greats were there. Graham once remarked that his supreme compliment came in the men's room at the Fillmore, while he was urinating. Two young guys entered and began pissing on either side of him. "Who's playing tonight?" asked the first. "I don't know, it doesn't matter. We're at the Fillmore!" replied the second.

Often accused of being a capitalist exploiter, Graham nonetheless personally maneuvered some of the biggest fundraising events of rock history, including Woodstock and Live Aid. After the Fillmore, he operated the Fillmore West in San Francisco and Fillmore East in New York, but San Francisco was always his base of operations. Married several times and devoted to his sons, Bill was a mensch with a heart of gold, and when he died untimely in a helicopter crash over the Bay Area in 1991, even his worst enemies were hard-pressed to say anything against him. Although he was hard-nosed and personally grasping of money and power, and hated for it, he revolutionized rock concerts and brought San Francisco its highest hour of musical prominence. Except for the City's opera tradition, Graham's rock shows may have been its pinnacle of musical greatness.

Certainly, no one has surpassed him since.

Weaving Spiders Come Not Here

Never has a club been more inaptly named than the Bohemian Club of San Francisco, operator of the Bohemian Grove on the Russian River seventy miles north of town, where every Republican president since Calvin Coolidge has come to play. It's hard to find anything remotely bohemian about this mostly white, all-male exclusive association of power brokers and heavy-hitting capitalists whose members include Henry Kissinger, George Bush, David Rockefeller, Henry Ford II, Stephen D. Bechtel Jr. of Bechtel Group, "Tom" Clausen, CEO of BankAmerica, and David Packard of Hewlett-Packard.

Herbert Hoover called it "the greatest men's party on earth." He referred to the annual two-week encampment at Bohemian Grove, where rich and powerful men gather to make complete fools of themselves, far from the scrutiny of the media or the nagging influence of their wives and mistresses.

Supposedly, these guys are not allowed to use the Grove camp for business or political ends; hence the club's motto, "Weaving spiders come not here." But give us all a break, does anybody believe that when Richard Nixon gave a speech around the campfire, it wasn't a political event? Dwight Eisenhower first announced his candidacy for president at Bohemian Grove, and it's said that Nelson Rockefeller dropped out of the 1964 race after his Bohemian speech failed to impress the membership.

There are twenty-three hundred members of the Bohemian Club, and not one of them is female. Blacks and Asians are represented in a tiny percentage, but otherwise the roster is lily white and archly conservative. There's a waiting list of thirteen years for Californians, eighteen years for non-Californians, to get in, and membership costs $8,500 in initiation fees and $110 a month in dues. Consider it an access fee of sorts, to be able to sit in a teepee with Merv Griffin or toast marshmallows with Barry Goldwater.

The Grove is set up very much like a boys' camp. It has tents, cabins, a lake, a mess hall. Oh, it also has a few amenities not found in any boys' camp, including servants, five-star French chefs, fine aged Scotch whiskey, medical facilities, an outdoor theater, a gourmet restaurant, parking attendants, its own post office, and a barber shop. No private telephones or radios or TVs are permitted, although harried executives and men of great power can use the pay phone booths for outgoing calls.

Deep into the hillside is an area called Cave Man's, the most exclusive neighborhood within this exclusive enclave. The tents and cabins become permanent, large homes here, and lowly regular members are not allowed to stroll in this vicinity without an invitation. Cave Men even eat in their own dining hall, with imported chefs preparing the feasts. Herbert Hoover and Richard Nixon were Cave Men; George Bush didn't make the grade.

Entertainment and performances are a big part of the Bohemian Grove tradition, so accomplished musicians and actors are admitted to the club as nonvoting "associate members," in exchange for which they donate their talents to the July extravaganza, on an outdoor stage, called the Grove Play.

Camp opens with an elaborate ritual in which a barge is floated across the lake and a mummy called "Care" is burned in effigy, symbolizing the idea that these guys are leaving their cares behind them. According to the Bohemian bible, "The Cremation of Care," the burning effigy indicates the "shedding from each of us of the snake's skin we grow in the workaday world . . . a dropping of the mask of pride, of position, or self-importance and greed and power. It cannot last, it is only for a spell, but it is a magic spell."

"It helps the American male, without discussing it, to cope with a very high-pressure world by giving him a time apart, a space apart," said historian Kevin Starr, a Bohemian regular. Starr is an intellectual, not an industrialist, but club membership has always included professors, authors, newspaper editors, and television anchors (Walter Cronkite, for one), people who are more influential than rich.

Every day at noon, a thousand men gather to sit on the grass and hear the Lakeside Talk. This "talk" is as often as not an important policy statement by a world leader or some significant announcement by a prominent thinker. Here, Nixon first discussed U.S.-Soviet detente, and Herbert Hoover delivered the acceptance of his Republican nomination. The Bohemian Grove has been a "networking" experience since long before that concept was invented. Men introduce themselves to each other, important conversations occur, and the high and mighty divide the spoils—while the hoi polloi fume and die outside the gates, unable to crack the camp's state-of-the-art security system, suitable even for heads of state.

Outside the gates in recent years have been long lines of picketers from the environmental, anti-war, liberal, radical, and women's rights constituencies. Members simply run this gauntlet and later joke about it among themselves.

The women finally made some small headway in 1988 when a court decision forced the Bohemian Club and the Grove to begin hiring women as waitresses. Some triumph. The fair sex has yet to crack the membership rolls, however, and may never do so. The exclusivity that prohibits women in the camp doesn't stop the members from going directly across the highway to patronize the services of prostitutes who fill the motels and do a land office business.

The last day of camp is reserved for the elaborate, one-time-only performance of the annual Grove Play. A cast of over a hundred amateurs and professionals parade around in silly costumes as tree sprites, noblemen, knights, monks, Indians, kilted Scots, kings, dukes, soldiers, and so forth. The "plot," such as it is, is predictable, with a macho ending in which the victorious royal personage is carried off by his loyal men. Fireworks explode in the sky, and a couple of thousand boozed-out, testosterone-oozing, mostly straight white guys all blubber and hug each other like some Robert Bly affinity group with money and power.

Those who are in on this little clique and its twenty-seven-hundred-acre playground swear by it for life, while the rest of us can only dream of such pleasures.

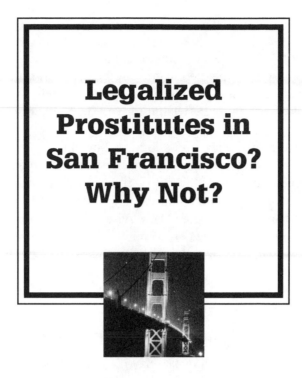

Legalized Prostitutes in San Francisco? Why Not?

It's a story that won't go away. Logic I: If prostitution can be legal in some parts of Nevada, there's clearly no federal law that would prevent its becoming legal in some parts of California. San Francisco, for example.

Logic II: If prostitution has always existed in San Francisco since its founding days, and 150 years of effort have utterly failed to eradicate it, then prohibition simply doesn't work. It may be against the law, but the law can't control it. It makes more sense to legalize the trade, in order to tax it for public benefit and protect the health of both the sex workers and their clients.

Logic III: If prostitutes in Amsterdam can be licensed, clean, open, honest, and government regulated, why not in San Francisco, the only American city with a prostitutes' labor union and annual Hookers' Ball?

"For all intents and purposes, prostitution is already legal," said one merchant along Polk Street. And he's right. The police make little effort to arrest prostitutes, and those who get busted are usually back on the streets within hours, after being cited and released on bail.

In 1994, City Supervisor Terrence Hallinan openly floated a proposal for San Francisco to operate city-run brothels, for both male and female whores, as a means to fight crime and impede the spread of AIDS. Would a prostitute be willing to work in a City bordello, however?

"As long as there's a spa and a Jacuzzi, I'm all for it," said transvestite prostitute "Jennifer Collins," interviewed on the street. "I'd rather pay ten percent to a brothel than to a pimp," he/she added.

"Unregulated prostitution causes major problems in San Francisco," Hallinan told the Board of Supervisors. Some of those problems occur in a neighborhood where Hallinan and his family own rental houses. "A way to get a handle on the problem . . . might be through legalization."

With street prostitution come drugs and crime, and the feeling is strong in San Francisco that if the City can legitimize its sex trade—move it indoors, so to speak—and regulate the industry, then the crime element will effectively disappear.

Neighborhood associations like Save Our Streets are strongly in favor of City brothels. Business leaders have endorsed the plan, too. Business in general suffers when whores take over the block. In fact, many people in San Francisco see the logic and good sense behind the idea, although Mayor Frank Jordan and religious leaders are still opposed.

The Board of Supervisors has set up a twenty-member committee (including three working prostitutes) to study the feasibility of the City bordello plan. "I don't know if people would go there," said one lady of the evening. "My clients don't want to be noticed."

While we await the outcome of the study, one thing is clear. If there is ever to be legal prostitution in a major American city, San Francisco will lead the way. The mere fact that the City is seriously considering this move indicates its complete surrender to the sex workers, its unwillingness to enforce any law against them. Prostitution will always be Job One there, even if it is never formally legalized.

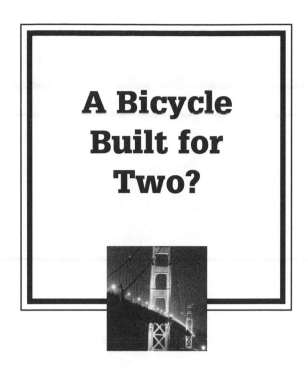

A Bicycle Built for Two?

It's hard to imagine how something as apparently sweet and innocuous as riding a bicycle could become controversial, political, even downright nasty, but in the Bay Area there are not one but two "bicycle wars" going on, and the combatants are plenty serious. In both San Francisco and Berkeley, a group called Critical Mass has taken over the streets and even the Bay Bridge, with hundreds of cyclists deliberately blocking traffic to cars, and numerous arrests following. Meanwhile, over the Golden Gate Bridge in lovely Marin County, bikers are pitted against hikers in a turf war over Mount Tamalpais's fragrant trails.

"We aren't blocking traffic," said Critical Mass founder David Cohen. "We *are* traffic." Police don't always agree.

"They call this a protest, but it's not a protest. It's a celebration. They don't call it a protest when they see a traffic jam on I-80. But I call that fossil fuelishness," Cohen added.

In San Francisco, the Critical Mass ride starts at Justin Herman Plaza on the last Friday of each month and regularly attracts about 800 participants on two-wheelers. The Berkeley ride is at rush hour (5:30 P.M.)

on the second Friday of the month and includes 150 to 300 bicyclists. Both rides are an outgrowth of the group called Auto Free Bay Area, a two-year-old advocacy organization opposed to the environmental and social poison of automobiles.

"We are poisoning the very things we need to survive," Cohen maintained. "All the things we need and love are being killed off by the toxic dumping of automobiles, including the air, the children, and the land."

Who are the Critical Massers? Some of them are long-haired, young protesters from other movements and causes, but others are gray-haired grannies and neatly attired Yuppies. They take no prisoners, offer no compromise. They ride together in a pack, using up all lanes of traffic and effectively barring the cars. While the stalled motorists fume about getting home late or their pizza getting cold, the bikers leaflet them with a brochure reading, "We know that *you* aren't responsible for the organization of our cities around motorized traffic, and if we have contributed to your delay, *we're sorry*. But maybe you can take this opportunity to reflect on what a world without cars would be like."

Seventy-three riders were arrested on Interstate 80, blocking the Bay Bridge rush hour commute. But in Berkeley at least, the police have pretty much given up trying to bust the riders. "What they're doing is illegal," said Officer Thomas Milner. "They are riding all over the place. You aren't allowed to do that. But we don't stop them anymore. We just treat it like a parade, like a special event."

It's also a fairly civilized form of civil disobedience. Except for a few rowdies who get carried away and spit on cars or scream at the cops, most of the cyclists are polite to the point of meek. They are not seeking confrontation so much as making their point, San Francisco style.

Over in Marin, things are a bit more heated. Mount Tamalpais is virtually a holy place, a mecca for walkers and hikers who have enjoyed its famous trails for generations. These folk are up in arms at the new generation of mountain bike enthusiasts who have taken over the trails, it's alleged, with high-speed, ecologically disturbing high jinks. The bikers claim they are simply enjoying nature; the hikers say the bikers are destroying it.

The principals in this war of bad blood are a forty-year-old builder of mountain bikes who claims to have invented the first successful such bike in his garage, named (yes) Joe Breeze, and an eighty-year-old Mill Valley potter and longtime Mount Tam hiker named Martin Friedman.

Here, too, the police are called in regularly. These cops are rangers from the Marin Municipal Water District, charged with policing the backwoods trails on the mountain, and they routinely pass out $200 citations to cyclists who exceed the officially posted speed limits, 15 mph on the straightaway and 5 mph on blind curves.

Ranger Gordon Hasler (yes) hassles the speeding bikers but doesn't much enjoy it. The cyclists, he complained, "have an attitude, like we're persecuting them or something. Some of them get hostile when we give them tickets, and they give us a lot of verbal abuse." The hikers tend to be older and more polite, but "they don't like us either. They always complain that we're not doing enough."

Both the Critical Mass and the mountain biker crowd have to be considered serious political forces in San Francisco terms. Great battles have been fought over less than the ownership of San Francisco and Berkeley streets or the winding trails of Mount Tam. And, in true San Francisco fashion, you can just about bet on the bicyclists to win out. They're new, they're hot, and they've got a valid point to make. Riding a bike shouldn't be considered anti-social activity while automobile traffic jams are taken for granted and pedestrian rights secured.

The Case of the Cop and the Dummy

Brendan O'Smarty is a dummy, notwithstanding his name. A little wooden fellow, he's the beat partner of San Francisco cop Bob Geary, fifty-three, who successfully defied Police Chief Anthony Ribera's order to ditch the puppet in the interest of authority and discipline.

It seems that Brendan upstaged one of Geary's superior officers at some kind of formal police function. Then it was departmental warfare against the dummy, culminating in the order that Geary would need written permission every time he took Brendan out of his trunk.

Geary fought back with a public proposition on the San Francisco ballot in November 1993 and won by a slim majority of votes. The dummy was saved, Brendan can again greet the children of San Francisco on the streets, and both the police chief and mayor ended up looking like humorless toads.

Indeed, the whole ballot measure came down to a question of humor—whether or not San Francisco still had enough whimsy to allow a cop to patrol the city with a puppet in hand or had become a city too serious for that. Whimsy won out.

Officer Geary spent $1,750 of his own money outfitting Brendan in

The Case of the Cop and the Dummy

This cop's no dummy: Police officer Bob Geary uses ventriloquist puppet Brendan O'Smarty to entertain and educate. (*AP/Wide World Photos*)

a perfect little cop's uniform mimicking his own, with a holster and tiny gun. Then he spent $10,000 getting the signatures necessary to put the Save Brendan proposition on the ballot. You could say this copper had a real love affair going with his pint-sized partner. He even took ventriloquy lessons.

"Now that Brendan is an in-law and not an outlaw, we can discuss his future," a victorious Geary said after the election. "If people think we're kooky, they're insulting democracy. . . . I hope there will be some kind of conciliation."

Mayor Frank Jordan remained unamused. "Hopefully, these kinds of measures will not be placed on the ballot in the future," he announced. (What kinds of measures? More puppet initiatives?) Comments from voters exiting the polls ranged from "It makes San Francisco look ridiculous" to "A lot of youths believe in the dummy."

The "Farley" cartoon strip in the *Chronicle* had a field day with the story ("If puppets are outlawed, only outlaws will have puppets!"). The world press ate it up, from Peking to Paris. And, of course, Herb Caen had the last word: in San Francisco politics, "a wooden personality is not a drawback."

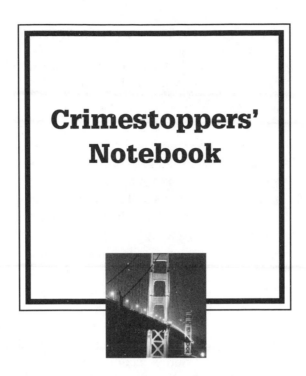

Crimestoppers' Notebook

They succeeded in robbing twenty-two banks in sixteen Bay Area cities in only five months, but they were no match for the Kid's angry mother. Police and FBI, using photos from the bank video monitors, had nicknamed the robbers Toothless (for the gap in his teeth) and the Kid, or Junior (for his apparent youth), who with a third conspirator had gained about $60,000, or an average of $2,700 a job, which they spent on drugs.

They were smart enough to avoid taking money tainted with exploding dye, and they never robbed banks close to their homes. But that was part of what got them caught. The cops made a map of where the twenty-two bank robberies had taken place and determined that one small circle in the center of Oakland was never hit, so the gang must live there.

Next, they put the robbers' pictures on television and identified the small area believed to be their home base. The Kid's mother went ballistic, seeing her son on TV like that, and she screamed at him until he called the police and turned himself in. Street people turned in the other two guys for the reward, but the Kid's mother declined payment. Just wanted to see her son go straight, she said.

The car bomb on May 24, 1990, tore the small Japanese sedan apart and grievously wounded its occupants, Darryl Cherney and Judi Bari, as the vehicle smashed into a steel barricade at Oakland High School. Two hours later, as Bari lay in intensive care at the hospital, fighting for survival, the Oakland police announced she had blown herself up.

Bari and Cherney were principals of a radical organization called Earth First! which had made its name as the most militant protest group defending the environment. Among other things, Earth First!ers were known to put spikes into northern California redwood trees, to create potentially lethal impediments to loggers. Police announced that since the car bomb was probably visible, the two radicals had meant to use it in some Earth First! protest.

The ensuing controversy engulfed the environmental movement in northern California, dividing the liberals from the radicals as well as the conservatives. Bari and Cherney claimed the bombing was an attack by an anti-abortion nut called "the Lord's avenger," or else the FBI itself had done it.

Nobody ever won the argument, and the charges were eventually dropped. Bari survived, but Earth First! tempered its activities, and the logging industry kept right on felling redwoods.

When Michael Covino's girlfriend woke him up at three in the morning saying "Someone is being mugged downstairs," he did what any good citizen of Berkeley might do. He opened the window, yelled down at the mugger (who was saying "Gimme your wallet or I'll shoot" to his intended victim) and fired his legal, registered .38 Smith & Wesson into the air to frighten off the criminal.

It worked. The would-be mugger ran off, jumping into a Honda Prelude waiting for him at the corner. A neighbor said, "Can you believe it? They're going around mugging people in a Prelude, not even a Civic or an Accord."

When Berkeley police arrived, however, Covino became the criminal. It's against the law in Berkeley to discharge a firearm in public. "We're not even allowed under Berkeley law to fire a warning shot," the cop told him. Worse yet, since he'd fired into the air, nobody knew where the bullet came down, a definite risk to the public welfare.

The gun was confiscated. The mugger was not.

Terror at 101 California Street

Reconstructing the carnage, it still seems hard to believe. Gian Luigi Ferri was a fifty-five-year-old mortgage broker who had run into some financial difficulties in his San Francisco–based company, money problems he blamed on poor legal advice from the firm of Pettit & Martin, located in the gleaming high-rise of 101 California Street.

Ferri wasn't known to be a violent man. He had a degree in psychology from the University of California at Santa Cruz and had spent several years working as a mental health counselor for Marin County's Department of Health and Human Services.

Nonetheless, on July 1, 1993, Ferri walked into the skyscraper carrying a black canvas bag containing two Intratec TEC-9 pistols, which could fire fifty times between loading, a semi-automatic .45 caliber handgun, and enough rounds of ammunition to kill a whole bunch of lawyers, which is exactly what he intended to do. The guns and ammo were legally purchased in Nevada under his real name. Ferri had been known to joke about killing lawyers, but who hasn't? That joke started with Shakespeare.

Calmly, he rode up to the thirty-fourth floor, entered the law offices, and opened fire. First to die were Jack Berman, thirty-five, a conscientious labor specialist, and his client, thirty-year-old Jody Sposato, the mother of an infant girl, who was suing a former employer for sexual discrimination.

As a secretary dialed 911 in response to the screams and gunshots, Ferri strode into the next office and murdered attorney Allen J. Berk, who was sitting at his desk, and critically wounded his partner, Brian Berger, who had been trying to warn Berk of the danger. While employees, clients, and lawyers all rushed for the stairwell and ran up to the thirty-fifth floor, Ferri ran down to the thirty-third and killed David Sutcliffe, thirty, a law student from the University of Colorado at Boulder who was visiting the City.

Spotting married couple John and Michelle Scully in the hallway, the gunman chased them into an adjoining office and murdered John, while the husband used his own body to shield his wife from harm.

Down another flight to the thirty-second floor, Ferri dispatched the lives of Shirley Mooser, sixty-four, a widow who worked as a secretary, Donald "Mike" Merrill, forty-eight, an investment specialist, and typist Deborah Fogel, thirty-three, who died asking people to take care of her dog.

After wounding several more people, the crazed mortgage broker found himself surrounded by approaching cadres of police, turned a gun on himself, and blew his own brains out. His assistant at the failed mortgage company, Tai Salisbory, said on hearing the news, "When they told me it was Gian, I couldn't believe it. You don't expect that from someone you know, no matter how lonely and sad and miserable he is."

The note police found in Ferri's bag ranted on and on about the bad lawyers at 101 California Street and how they had screwed him. The gunman also had theories about the toxic effects of MSG in food and was a devotee of San Francisco–based televangelist Reverend Terry Cole-Whittaker, whose slogan was "Prosperity—Your Divine Right."

The firm of Pettit & Martin later announced it would lobby Congress and the White House for stricter controls on semi-automatic weapons, but it's too late for the victims of the high-rise massacre by the Bay.

Lesbian Avengers Wield Weenies, Bobbitt Style

Remember the case of Lorena Bobbitt, who cut off her husband John's penis with a carving knife and threw it away in a field? Well, the Lesbian Avengers of Berkeley remembered her when they staged a "Bobbit-que" and offered "barbequed penis" (actually nutritious turkey franks) for sale on the busy corner of Shattuck and Virginia.

It was a protest, of course. The corner of Virginia Street was chosen because the Bobbitt severed-penis case happened in Manassas, Virginia, "a state where a man can rape his wife with impunity," said Avenger and chef Katie Hern. "Yes means yes, no means no, or else that penis has got to go," the lesbians chanted.

Some women onlookers seemed amused, but men tended to walk by as quickly as possible. "Barbequed penis, sir?" one of the lesbians asked a passerby. "Already have one!" one fellow replied.

Somebody called the Berkeley police to chase away these rabidly anti-male weenie roasters, but officer Rick Mosher reported he could do nothing since the women were not using an open flame (a Berkeley no-no) but had heated the plump, juicy "members" beforehand in a crockpot.

Lesbian Avengers protest a local school board's decision to reject a multicultural curriculum, 1992. (*AP/Wide World Photos*)

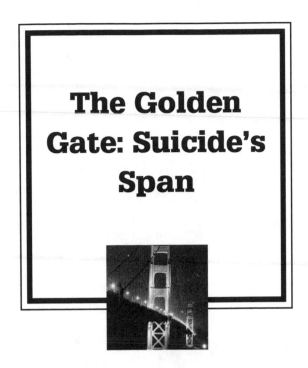

The Golden Gate: Suicide's Span

There is simply no more popular place to kill yourself than the Golden Gate Bridge, no more stylish way to do it. Jumping off the great orange span, free-falling 265 feet into the Pacific, at a speed of seventy-five miles per hour in about four seconds, is so compelling to people that at least 938 of them have done it since the bridge opened in 1937. The actual figure is doubtless much higher, including those who were never seen and bodies never found.

On average, somebody jumps off the Golden Gate Bridge every three weeks. And at least four people try to jump for every one who succeeds in doing it. Some who are cajoled from committing suicide and dragged off to psychiatric wards just keep coming back, trying again and again until they fly.

Why? Partly, its the mystique. Those rare jumpers (approximately 2 percent) who survived to talk about it had comments like: "It was a romantic thing to do." "It was sure death in a painless fashion." "I was attracted to the bridge—an affinity between me, the Golden Gate Bridge, and death—there is a kind of form to it, a certain grace and beauty."

The Golden Gate Bridge under construction, 1936. (*Bettmann*)

The Golden Gate: Suicide's Span

The bridge's chief engineer and great promoter, Joseph Strauss, was a diminutive Chicagoan who loved to take on awesome, world-challenging projects. He promised San Francisco the bridge would be safe from suicide in an article published a year before it opened. "The Golden Gate Bridge is practically suicide proof. The intricate telephone and patrol systems will operate so efficiently that anyone acting suspiciously would be immediately surrounded. Suicide from the bridge is neither possible nor probable," Strauss wrote. Despite intense opposition from the military, barge and ferry owners, the Southern Pacific Railroad, and the banks (fearful of the cost), Strauss was able to win over the voters of San Francisco to issue bonds for construction of this world-famous span, as ethereal as it is mighty.

Only three months after the bridge opened in 1937 with a "Pedestrians Day" swarm of two hundred thousand walkers crossing it, it claimed its first victim. Harold Wobber was a World War I vet. He fought off a bystander who tried to restrain him, scaled the three-and-a-half-foot-high fence, and plunged to his death below.

Others followed. And how. The Eiffel Tower in Paris was the only competition for the world's number one suicide location, but the French constructed suicide barriers on it in 1968, and no one has succeeded in jumping off since then. Interestingly enough, as of that year, the Eiffel Tower and the Golden Gate Bridge had chalked up exactly the same number of suicides, 352. But the tower in Paris got a much earlier start, in 1889. Since 1968, the bridge's "superiority" in numbers has grown so inordinately that it now seems no place will ever match its record.

Over the years, many suicide prevention agencies have lobbied the city to install an effective barrier, but nobody wants to lose the spellbinding view of the City and sea from the bridge. There is now a plan afoot to install telephones directly linked to a twenty-four-hour suicide prevention hotline, but experts agree that won't solve the problem completely. "The bridge is like a loaded gun on your coffee table. If we really want to save lives, we have to unload that gun," said Dr. Jerome Motto of the University of California at San Francisco, a psychiatrist and suicide authority.

The people who work at the gift shop on the south end of the bridge, the San Francisco side, are spooked. They actually see the bodies falling when looking out the shop window. They hear the screams.

Roy L. Raymond, the feisty entrepreneur who started the Victoria's Secret ladies' lingerie chain in San Francisco, was a recent suicide off the Golden Gate. In August 1993, he drove his Toyota to the middle of the span, left notes for his wife and children, and took the dive. Raymond was a self-made millionaire, a man others would call brilliant and successful, but he couldn't resist the allure of that foggy plunge in the predawn mist of poetry and sadness.

Roy Raymond had a way with visions. He started Victoria's Secret on a shoestring because he had found himself embarrassed while trying to buy his wife a slip in a regular department store. From the beginning, it was a ladies' lingerie store for men. It was naughty, risqué, perfectly San Francisco, a store selling sex in the delicate guise of a Victorian boudoir, a classy version of Frederick's of Hollywood.

Within a year, Victoria's Secret had sales of half a million dollars, and in five years the original store had grown to a chain of five outlets, all in the Bay Area. At that time, in 1982, Raymond was bought out of the business by The Limited and received about $4 million. Victoria's Secret went nationwide and now has over five hundred outlets and a mail order catalog. Roy Raymond went home and cooked up new ideas.

He started a store called My Child's Destiny, selling expensive children's toys and computer games to Yuppie parents, but went bankrupt after two years. He also lost money on a children's bookstore called Quinby's. By 1990, he was broke, and by 1993, dead.

Friends described a man who was unbowed by business failures and eternally optimistic, yet something of an unrealistic dreamer. When the IRS filed a garnishment of $77,000 against him, three days before his death, he may have snapped. The bridge called out. The bridge was waiting there, accessible and inviting. Another heart left in San Francisco, another genius doused in the roiling waters of the Bay.

A Slow
News Day

It was a beautiful idea, it really was, and so what if it was completely impractical. San Franciscans bought it in a big way, and for a few weeks it was the hottest thing going.

The idea: casino gambling on Alcatraz Island as a scheme to raise $150 million in annual revenue to offset the City's budget deficit.

The schemer: Warren Hinckle, columnist for the *Examiner*. Hinckle has been a famous character in the City since way back in the 1960s, when he was one of the founders of *Ramparts* magazine. He sports a stylish figure with his ample girth, black eyepatch, and omnipresent basset hound, Bentley. Sort of a cross between Art Buchwald and Hunter S. Thompson, Hinckle is a talented writer and enough of a nut that you can't know when to take him seriously.

But he managed to convince the voters of San Francisco to put his casino proposal on the ballot. His idea, in short, was for San Francisco to compete with Reno and Las Vegas and turn the godforsaken rock and former penitentiary into a glittering casino and hotel, a tourist destination. The *Examiner* ran a popular poll, which found the citizenry in favor of the idea by a margin of two to one. The merchants

The eternal mystique of Alcatraz Island, 1969. (*Bettmann*)

on Fisherman's Wharf, standing to gain, were all for it. Hinckle included the casino proposal as part of his 1988 mayoral campaign.

"The ugly duckling of Alcatraz may be a pot of gold for San Francisco, desperately in search of a rainbow," Hinckle crowed in his column.

The only thing wrong with the idea was everything about it. For starters, the California state constitution doesn't allow casino gambling, except on Native American reservations. Otherwise, why would anyone have gone to the wasteland deserts of Nevada to throw money away on craps? For Alcatraz to have a casino would require nothing less than a constitutional amendment, a real long shot because of Sacramento lobbyists representing an anti-casino coalition that includes such unlikely allies as Christian fundamentalists and racetrack owners.

A Slow News Day

Second, Alcatraz belongs to the federal government, not to San Francisco. Specifically, it's a national park. The City would have to convince Congress to pass a law deeding the property over, essentially surrendering national recreational parkland for a gambling operation. The whole concept is "ludicrous," according to the director of the National Park Service, William Mott Jr. "Alcatraz is a national treasure. It belongs to the people, not to San Francisco. If a lease were proposed, we would answer with a very positive and very forceful 'No!' " he said.

Finally, experts agreed that Hinckle's estimate of $150 million a year in profits was simply way off the mark. Even the biggest casinos in the world don't produce that much in city revenues.

Hinckle's fellow *Examiner* columnist Rob Morse paid him a kind of backhand compliment, however, writing that "it's really amazing how many suckers the casino has attracted, and it hasn't even opened yet."

The last word, or course, was left to Herb Caen, who commended dryly that it was a "fine idea for Hinckle on a slow news day."

Hankerin'
for You

The Official San Francisco Hanky Code below has now been adopted by heterosexuals as well as gays. You can wear your hanky anywhere on your body, but the most popular place to display one is tucked into your back pants pocket. The most important thing is which side of your body you wear it on, since opposite sides indicate opposite sexual propensities, to wit:

Color of Hanky	On Left	On Right
Paisley	Wearing boxer shorts	Looking for boxer shorts
Checkered	Safe sex top	Safe sex bottom
White lace (women)	Victorian top	Victorian bottom
Chamois	Motorcyclist	Looking for biker
Orange	Anything goes	Not tonight, dear
Leopard	Tattooed	Goes for tattoos
Gray	Wears a suit	Gets off on suits

Hankerin' for You

Color of Hanky	On Left	On Right
Apricot	Fat	Likes 'em chubby
Charcoal	Dildo-wielding top	Dildo-taking bottom
Silver lamé	Looking for celebrity	Celebrity
Mosquito netting	Outdoor top	Outdoor bottom
Cocktail napkin	Bartender	Barfly

Supervisors and Mayor Go to Pot (for Medical Purposes)

It became official November 24, 1993. The City and County of San Francisco formally announced its belief in the use of marijuana for compassionate, medical purposes and ordered the police department to consider the prosecution of those growing or using pot for medical purposes as its lowest priority. In effect, unless all the muggers, rapists, burglars, and killers in San Francisco decide to become law-abiding citizens, the cops will never have time to chase after pot-growing people with AIDS.

In three resolutions signed by the supervisors and mayor, San Francisco went on record urging both the state and federal governments to abolish their laws against medical use of marijuana and established a commission to discuss further medicinal uses of pot, including as a tool in alcohol and hard-drug abuse problems.

The San Francisco policy is easily the most liberal in the nation. Down in San Diego in 1994, an AIDS patient was jailed for sixteen months without bail for growing pot in his backyard to alleviate his nausea and other symptoms like those that killed his lover. But even the U.S. government, taking note of the San Francisco experiment, has begun studies that may lead to liberalization of the pot laws.

There seems no question of the beneficial effects smoking or ingesting THC (the principal chemical ingredient in marijuana) has on victims of AIDS, breast cancer, glaucoma, or chemotherapy. The magical ingredient eases nausea and combats weight loss in patients suffering from "wasting syndrome," so that the pot itself improves life expectancy as well as making the patient more comfortable. The only major exception is people with the lung disease pneumocystis, for whom any kind of smoking is hazardous and toxic, but these patients can get THC from the drug Marinol, essentially marijuana in pill form,

AIDS activists March on Gay Pride Day in San Francisco, 1983.
(*Bettmann*)

or eat it in brownies and pastries such as those served to AIDS patients by San Francisco's own Brownie Mary, the Mother Teresa of the AIDS ward.

Even before the pro-pot resolutions passed, Brownie Mary was golden in the Golden Gate. Although she openly admitted baking and distributing the pot brownies to AIDS patients, she was acquitted of any crime by a San Francisco jury.

In compelling testimony, the chair of the Board of Supervisors, Angela Alioto, said she knew at least one person who used pot for pain relief in a terminal disease: her own husband, who died of stomach cancer.

Although you can't exactly go to San Francisco and blow a joint on the steps of City Hall as people did in the heady Summer of Love, it's still true that the City has the most permissive and tolerant attitude toward the drug of all U.S. cities, rivaling even Amsterdam and Bangkok in its open acceptance. "Everybody" knows about the marijuana supermarket for AIDS patients operated by longtime hemp activist Dennis Peron and his fellow believers. The PBS depiction of landlady Anna Madrigal taping a joint to her tenant's door in Armistead Maupin's "Tales of the City" was amusing because it was true to life, so believable in the City that dreams and that cares for its ill and dying.

Paper Boy

Everybody knows the City has two newspapers, both established in the late nineteenth century, the *Chronicle* and the *Examiner*. The former has long been the leader in circulation and is published in the morning, while the *Examiner* is the afternoon paper and a distant second banana, until Sunday comes and both *Chron* and *Ex* join forces in a merged edition.

What most people don't know is that the *Chronicle* started out as a review of current plays in the City, under the name *Daily Dramatic Chronicle*, and that the *Examiner* was a failing throwaway sheet until in 1887 George Hearst gave it to his ne'er-do-well son, William Randolph Hearst, as a twenty-fourth birthday present. Some say the *Chronicle*, notorious for its tabloid-style scandal-and-sex reportage, should still be called the *Daily Dramatic Chronicle*. Meanwhile, the contemporary *Examiner* is still published by William Randolph Hearst, number III, and some say it's still a failing throwaway sheet.

The *Chronicle* was founded by brothers Charles and Michael de Young, who had emigrated to the City from St. Louis in 1850 and realized by 1865 that San Francisco had enough theatrical productions to warrant a full-scale play-reviewing newspaper. It started out as a free broadsheet. Then it branched into news and volatile, provocative editorials penned by Charles de Young, who once so enraged a mayoral candidate that the candidate's son stormed the *Chronicle* office and killed the editor.

Willy Hearst at twenty-four years old was a spoiled brat just thrown out of Harvard, who took on the *Examiner* as a kind of toy. Something to keep the kid busy. He plunged into a kind of histrionic journalism that would come to be known as "Hearst style." His first issue's headline read "Dead Babies: Bloody Work: More Ghastly Light on the Slaughter of the Innocents: The Dark Mysteries of a Great City." A house fire was not simply a blaze, it was a "great, searing conflagration." A rival art critic to the *Examiner*'s own Ambrose Bierce was not just a fool but "an anile and unhaired wretch."

When the news wasn't sensational enough, *Examiner* writers were known to go out and create some news on their own. A reporter might jump into San Francisco Bay to generate a headline like "Eaten by Sharks." One loose cow at a picnic became "Bovine Terror."

Of course, William Randolph Hearst became a legend and begat William Junior, who begat William the Third, and also the Hearst Castle in San Simeon, Patricia Hearst's abduction into the Symbionese Liberation Army, and today's Hearst Syndicate newspaper network. Orson Welles's film *Citizen Kane* was loosely based on the exploits of WRH2.

Willy 3 now stars in an *Examiner* TV commercial in which he drives an *Examiner* delivery van and scoops up two quarters from an old lady on the street, in exchange for "today's news today," the *Examiner* pitch for an afternoon paper. In reality, of course, afternoon newspapers have gone the way of the barber pole in American life. Only a few cities still have one. TV delivers the urgent news more swiftly, while the morning paper provides reflection on yesterday's events.

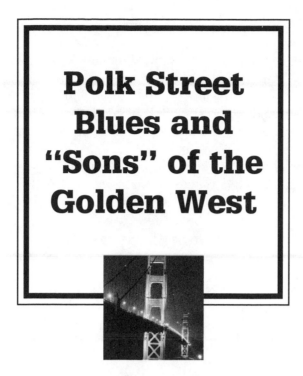

Polk Street Blues and "Sons" of the Golden West

$\mathbf{T}$he corner of Polk Street and Austin Alley is known as "Hustler Heaven" in the City, a place where men go to pick up boy prostitutes. But Patrick Kirk, twenty-eight, says he wasn't soliciting when four men gang-raped him the night of March 10, 1994, in a scene right out of a gay porno fantasy film.

Kirk had left the Q.T. bar around 11 P.M. when he was assaulted in the alley. The quartet forced him to the ground, pulled his pants down, and took turns raping him, Kirk told San Francisco police.

After the four raced off, Kirk tried in vain to telephone the City's rape-victim assistance lines for help. "Some weren't open, some didn't deal with men, and some put me on hold for so long that I just hung up," he said.

Frustrated, Kirk got a taxi to the San Francisco airport, filed a police report there, and flew down to his mother's house in Los Angeles in the middle of the night, finding medical attention at an emergency room clinic in the Southland.

Would he go back to Polk Street? Sure. "I am gay, but anal sex is not something I do. I don't like that. I want people to realize that rape happens to men [in San Francisco]," Kirk said. "It's important to seek help immediately." Even if it means going to L.A.

According to an account published by an anonymous Son of Bacchus, the all-male orgy is still alive in San Francisco and in fact has reached new heights (or depths, depending on your attitude) in this fin de siècle.

The new Sons of Bacchus are a mysterious group who stage a monthly Saturday night orgy for a hundred men "of all ages, colors, and physical types" at private homes in the City. The location is not announced until an hour beforehand, then everybody meets in one place for busing to another, usually a mansion in Pacific Heights or some other venue capable of entertaining a crowd. Invitations are sought after and envied.

The orgy is planned to last four hours, after which the guests are returned to their mundane real lives in a fleet of taxicabs. Rather than inviting only buffed porno stars or pretty boys, the organizers look for "guys who are open sexually, adventurous, and respect the other person's body."

But what about HIV and AIDS? Condoms and spermicidal lubes are available in great quantity, and the men are enjoined to "behave as if everyone here is HIV-positive." Monitors check for unsafe sexual behavior and would expel anyone who performed it, but according to legend, everyone acts properly.

So to speak. There are guys rolling around on the floor, they're all naked or wearing only a towel (having checked their clothes at the door), and every kind of sex, paired off and in groups, goes on publicly.

The orgy officially begins with an opening ceremony not unlike the Olympics, with robes, masks, and gongs. A massive den is covered in fake black leather and sports beanbag chairs. The kitchen is a popular place for "counter sex." The garden accommodates healthy, outdoors types, and some people, gluttons for privacy, hide out in the bathrooms. "Breakfast" is served at 2:30 A.M., then the guests are hustled off.

"I got waylaid, relaid, and rondelaid," said a man who called himself Tom Bacchus. But how one garners an invitation to these affairs remains an absolute mystery. Nobody will talk about the invitation process, but it seems to help if you belong to certain Castro-area gyms, play in the gay softball league, or write a gossip column for one of the rags.

Meanwhile, controversial plans are underway to open a new bathhouse in the Tenderloin, although the gay baths were shut down in San Francisco in the mid-1980s because of the AIDS epidemic. The new facility under construction at 132 Turk Street is owned by the proprietors of the Steamworks in Berkeley, which never closed despite the plague. Regulations now require that cubicles have no doors and that lighting be bright, but the Sons of Bacchus have shown that in San Francisco you can't stop the fellows from fraternizing at will.

Pebble Beach Babylon

It started out as a vacation getaway for the rich and idle of San Francisco and has wound up as a vacation getaway for the rich and idle of the world. Pebble Beach today is a gated, private resort community one hundred miles south of the City on the Monterey Peninsula, home of the most famous golf courses in the country, a prized property that changes hands between American and Japanese billionaires every few years and is so ritzy that ordinary tourists must pay $5.50 just for the privilege of driving through it.

Originally known as Del Monte Forest, Pebble Beach is a residential community covering fifty-three hundred acres, with seventy-four miles of privately maintained roads, twenty-six hundred families, seven major golf courses, some of the most spectacular coastline in California (including the celebrated Lone Cypress tree overlooking the Pacific) and the ultra-luxurious Lodge at Pebble Beach and Inn at Spanish Bay, the latter constructed in the 1980s over the horrified protests of environmentalists and locals.

But ordinary locals don't live at Pebble Beach or have any sway. This place is for the likes of Marvin Davis, who owned it with 20th

Century Fox, and Tokyo industrialists who scandalized the community by trying to institute million-dollar membership fees for the use of the greens. The grass is certainly green here, even if the environmental spirit is not. It helps to say "Clint Eastwood sent me."

The historical antecedent to the Pebble Beach Company was the old Hotel Del Monte in Monterey, opened in 1880. It cost over a million dollars, accommodated five hundred guests, and was simply the most elegant place for San Francisco high society to go. After coming down from the City by train, visitors would board a stagecoach for the so-called Seventeen Mile Drive through Pacific Grove and Pebble Beach, south to the ancient Carmel Mission, and back to Monterey. In 1908, the Pebble Beach Lodge was built as a stopover place for people taking this roundtrip tour through what has been rightly called the greatest meeting of land and sea in the world.

In February 1919, the Del Monte Properties Company (the predecessor of Pebble Beach Corp.) was formed by Samuel F. B. Morse, the grandnephew of the inventor of the telegraph, who became the "Duke of Del Monte," presiding over the Hotel Del Monte, Pebble Beach Lodge, and seven thousand acres of choice land. He loved horses, sailing, and golf and oversaw the opening of the first Pebble Beach course in 1919, the Cypress Point course in 1928, Spyglass Hill in 1966, and Spanish Bay in 1986.

Along the way, Morse made a number of enemies and instituted the policy of charging admission at the toll gates to anyone not privileged enough to live at Pebble Beach. This toll continues to irritate and exclude the masses and raise the thorny issue of how these power-playing industrialists managed to nab the most beautiful coastline in northern California and take it away from any kind of public access. Virtually every other foot of beach in California is either publicly owned or accessible to people without a fee.

Morse's ruthless wheelings and dealings eventually forced out his partner, Herbert Fleishacker, during the Great Depression, and Morse prospered because he'd had the foresight to acquire the Monterey County Water Works, which he sold back to the people in 1930 for enough money to own all of Pebble Beach without debts. In 1946, he sold the Hotel Del Monte to the U.S. Navy for its Naval Postgraduate School and moved his hotel and resort operations into Pebble Beach for keeps.

The superb golf courses proved to be the area's greatest asset, even to the present day when Japanese corporate honchos vie for the right to play there. In the 1940s, crooner Bing Crosby moved his annual Pro-Am Tournament to Pebble Beach from southern California and began the February tradition of "the clambake," so ingrained in Monterey consciousness that the weather in February is always referred to as "Crosby weather." But Bing's widow, Kathryn Crosby, had a big falling out with the tournament directors in 1985 and refused to let them use his name any longer, so the event is now called the AT&T Pro-Am, which doesn't have the same cachet. Bing and Kathryn built their palatial estate in Hillsborough, just south of San Francisco, where she resides still, issuing regal proclamations.

Samuel F. B. Morse died in 1969, after half a century of lording it over this private reserve. The largest open space in the Del Monte Forest is now the eighty-four-acre S.F.B. Morse Botanical Reserve, bordering the neighbor town of Carmel. In 1977, Del Monte Properties changed its name to Pebble Beach Corporation, registered in Delaware, and by 1979 the whole thing belonged to 20th Century Fox Film Corporation, which sold out to Japan in the heady megabucks era of the late 1980s. One thing that has never changed is that Pebble Beach is still the place where the limitlessly rich of San Francisco can hide out for the weekend, drinking and playing their favorite sports.

The Forest no longer excludes people because they are black or Jewish, but it still takes plenty of money to buy a home in Pebble Beach, and you will find few examples of ethnic diversity there. Even some Monterey and Carmel residents—next-door neighbors, so to speak—will never set foot in the Forest, because they're insulted by the admission fee. Samuel Morse defended the toll saying that "without the charges, the area would have become like the rest of the waterfront on the California coast, uncontrolled and spoiled." Other people say it's just because of greed, racism, and the desire to eliminate "undesirables."

Speaking of neighboring Carmel, there's no charge for entering the town, but you'd better be prepared to part with big bucks if you want to eat or stay there. Since actor/producer/land developer/tycoon Clint Eastwood was elected mayor in April 1986, Carmel has received more free publicity than any village of three thousand residents anywhere

Clint Eastwood, who won the Carmel mayoral race by a landslide, hams it up for news photographers, 1986. (*Bettmann*)

in the world. Some locals even organized a bumper sticker campaign around the theme "Save Carmel—Impeach Clint."

The village has street names, but the houses have no numbers. Everyone in town must pick up his or her mail at the central post office. The tiny, narrow streets are dripping with charm and packed with boutiques, antique shops, art galleries tending toward moody seascapes, pretentious little restaurants with Continental airs, bars that have the atmosphere of a private club, sidewalks that abruptly end in sand, and great old cypress trees sometimes embedded right in the middle of the street. It's against the law to cut a tree in Carmel, even if it threatens the foundation of your home. There are no streetlights or fast food joints, in deference to the quaint and expensive nature of the place.

Clint Eastwood's restaurant is called the Hog's Breath Inn—how charmant—and is next door to an office building he developed after being elected mayor and sidestepping the difficulties he'd had with an earlier city council. In fact, Eastwood as much as admitted he ran for office only to further his own real estate ambitions, and after one term he quickly stepped down. He also restored and reopened the vast, historic Mission Ranch saloon, restaurant, and hotel near the mission.

Now Pebble Beach and Carmel await you, the San Francisco visitor with time and money to burn, if you need a place where absolute decadence is the rule and even the easy-going ways of the City seem tame.

New Age Nudies

There's a curious kind of aristocracy in northern California, unlike anything in L.A. It places a high value on New Age mysticism, naturism, nudity, Oriental thought and massage, and "roughing it" in style at the coastal and mountain retreats within day-tripping reach of San Francisco. The favored spots for those who can afford them are Big Sur, the Esalen Institute, Carmel Valley, an the Tassajara Zen Center, an offshoot of the San Francisco Zendo hidden deep in the Los Padres National Forest.

Big Sur has always had its own community, decadent lifestyle, insular detachment from the civilized world, and famous, rich hedonists. The novelist Henry Miller probably did as much as anyone to publicize this coastal paradise, writing such books as *Big Sur and the Oranges of Hieronymous Bosch* while practicing his lascivious tastes on the local maidens. Jack Kerouac wrote a novel called *Big Sur*, but he actually spent only a few weeks there. He stayed in a cabin owned by Lawrence Ferlinghetti, feverishly running back and forth up to San Francisco to get drunk with his Beat pals.

Today, no mere writer could afford a pad in Big Sur. Ted Turner and Jane Fonda have a vacation house there, John Denver spends some time in his picturesque A-frame overlooking the crashing Pacific, and some local residents even send their chauffeurs up to Carmel, a twenty-mile drive over a narrow road clinging to the side of cliffs, to pick up each day's *Wall Street Journal.*

The favored place to eat is still Nepenthe, meaning "land of no regrets," and you'll understand why after enjoying their ambrosia burger with a basket o' fries big enough for four people and four rap-scallion blue jays, washed down with their famous Tequila Sunset, which is a Tequila Sunrise with a jigger of 151-proof rum added and *pow* that's it, you're *gone.* It's remarkable that anyone can drive that coast highway after drinking even one, and sure enough every year a couple of foolish people go headlong off the cliffs into the briny deep.

If you're so inclined and willing to spend at least $300 a night, you can check into the Ventana Inn, which like Nepenthe is a venerable Big Sur institution. The rooms are all quite luxurious although very rustic (no television, puhleeze), and the restaurant is justly famous for its superb cuisine and magnificent wine list, all at smack-up-to-date prices.

Just a whisper down the coast from here is the world-renowned Esalen Institute, where you shouldn't go if you're offended by nudity, or indeed unless you plan to take all your own clothes off. Suitably undressed, you may sit in the hot tubs with some of the richest and most powerful CEOs, movie stars, psychics, plastic surgeons, shrinks, and saints in the world. More than one best-selling book or seminar scam has been cooked up in those steaming waters.

Don't think that you can just drive on in to Esalen, however. They charge plenty for their encounter weekends and seminars, and you do need a ticket and an appointment, although the hot tubs are open to the public (for a reasonable admission fee) on certain days between the hours of midnight and dawn. Call ahead and find out. Bring your own condoms and wine.

In Carmel Valley, which stands behind these coastal extravagances, you find a class of reclusive millionaires and holy men. You might, for example, drive past the locked gates of Merv Griffin's palatial estate, where he lived with his male companion who later sued him for pal-imony. (They were often seen together drinking at the Clock Garden restaurant and lounge in Monterey, according to owner Bob Canon, who also founded Monterey's only gay bar, the After Dark, but Griffin denied having anything but an employer-employee relationship with the fellow.)

If you drive far enough into the Valley, and just about destroy the shock absorbers on your car, you may eventually arrive at the Tassajara Zen Center, a place for the truly elite of San Francisco's New Age community. Even though it might be only twenty miles from Carmel as the crow flies, it takes three hours to drive there over an unpaved back road that is deliberately kept in horrible condition. You can only go in the summer, as Tassajara slams its gates to outsiders on Labor Day.

Here, too, there is a prevailing standard of chic nakedness, although the Zen monks have seen fit to provide a ladies-only side of the natural baths for women who don't care to be ogled by gents. There is no electricity or plumbing at Tassajara, but they do have a telephone and manage to bake the world's most delicious bread using only the wood-fired ovens. The whole experience is sublimely out of this world, although you might worry a bit about what could happen in the event of a medical emergency, or whether or not your car is going to survive the return trip to town.

Zen monks take no vows of chastity like their Christian counterparts, so pretty much anything goes once you get lost at Tassajara. You'll be lucky to get back to San Francisco at all.

E Pluribus Unum?

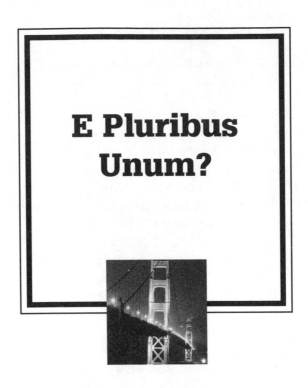

For many years, the choicest piece of San Francisco real estate, some fifteen hundred acres directly overlooking the Golden Gate Bridge, has belonged to the U.S. Army. Originally a fort, it's called the Presidio Army Base. But with the downsizing of the military in the '90s, the army has been gradually taking leave of the place, and of course that has opened up a free-wheeling, zany, no-holds-barred competition among San Francisco special interest groups who want to take over the land.

Among the suggestions:

- The Muwekma Ohlone Indians, all 150 of them, threaten to exercise their ancestral right to the land and make it into a reservation.
- A wacky and terrifically entertaining group called the Pickle Family Circus wants to make the Presidio the site of a three-ring circus, permanently ensconced.
- Bungee-jumping enthusiasts would like to use the Presidio as a staging ground for bungee jumps off the Golden Gate Bridge and

the "ejector seat," which catapults the adventuresome athlete into thin air over the Bay.

- Militant nudists want access to more nude beaches, disregarding the fact that the Presidio is too damn cold even when you're fully clothed, and it is swathed in thick fog year round.
- Animal rights activists want a nature preserve safe for all living things, while university researchers want a laboratory in which they can conduct torturous experiments on animals.
- Advocates for the homeless want the abandoned army barracks turned into housing for those who need it.
- Windsurfers want free access to some of the best—that is, windiest—coastline in the world, *and* they demand free parking.
- The army itself wants to retain exclusive use of its championship eighteen-hole golf course, while the National Park Service argues that the course should be open to the public, with greens fees helping to pay for the upkeep.
- Skunk lovers want the natural habitat of the Presidio skunks to be left unmolested.
- A Republican congressman from Tennessee, John J. Duncan, calls all these ideas "an absurd boondoggle" and wants the government to sell off the land to private, big-bucks developers. "He's making us out to be a bunch of far-out bizarros," said a Presidio Park spokesperson.

Far-out bizarros? In San Francisco, it takes more than the above suggestions to be classified as such.

No Business Like Slow Business

As San Francisco complains of an exhausted city budget and huge deficit, and the numbers of homeless continue to rise while public services and civility decline, there are those who say the City is only getting its just deserts. This is a place that has been downright unfriendly to business since the wacky, wacky days of Emperor Norton and his personally issued scrip.

While Art Agnos was mayor in 1991, Board of Supervisors member Bill Maher said, "What you have is a mayor who believes that management is the way the powerful oppress the weak, an electorate of largely transient voters who believe capitalism is a crime, and a Board of Supervisors who represent those beliefs. It's self-destructive lunacy."

Consider:

- A homeless person needs to reside only three days in San Francisco in order to qualify for a General Assistance check of $340 a month. This generous policy, by far the most liberal in California, has caused neighboring cities to put their homeless people on one-way bus rides to San Francisco.

No Business Like Slow Business

- San Francisco added more than one hundred thousand jobs to its employment base in the 1970s, but in the 1980s only fourteen thousand new jobs were created.
- When the City declared itself a sanctuary for war resisters and conscientious objectors during the Persian Gulf War, the American Petroleum Institute called off two conventions scheduled to take place there, costing San Francisco more than $7 million in lost revenue.
- The supervisors in 1986 voted to stop buying gas from the Chevron Corporation, San Francisco's biggest business, because Chevron had interests in South Africa. The huge company retaliated by moving thousands of its employees to outlying suburban areas.
- Growth-control laws prohibit new construction in the City over 750,000 square feet per year. When Wells Fargo Bank wanted to consolidate its operations into a new downtown office building, it couldn't get past the draconian restrictions and finally gave up trying.
- San Francisco has one public employee for every 29 residents. Compare that to Los Angeles, with one for every 76, Oakland with one for 85, and San Jose one for 142. San Francisco's public employees are union members earning the highest pay in California and 43 percent more than federal employees in comparable positions.
- Although the idea was ultimately shot down, the supervisors proposed to declare San Francisco a sanctuary for sexual minorities, with road signs stating as much on the highways entering town.
- Pacific Telesis paid $720 per employee in business taxes in San Francisco, $240 per employee in L.A., $120 in Oakland, and $10 in San Jose.
- The upshot: San Francisco is a great place to be if you don't care about, or are actively hostile toward big business, or if you're a practicing socialist. It's not the most difficult or most expensive U.S. city to do business in, however. That distinction belongs to New York, with its one public employee for every twenty-one citizens.

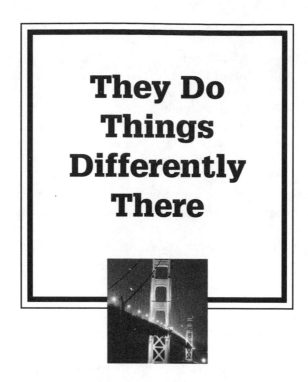

They Do Things Differently There

If you think there are all kinds of people in New York, you're right. Jersey City, New Jersey, has a wide variety, too. But what's the most ethnically diverse place in the country? San Francisco, of course, and by a long shot, according to a demographic study at Cal State in Northridge.

Professors James Allen and Eugene Turner ranked the ethnic makeup of every metropolitan region with over ten thousand residents. They found that the four most diverse counties in the United States are all in or adjoining San Francisco—San Francisco, San Mateo, Alameda, and Santa Clara counties. The most populous subgroups are Asian (Japanese, Chinese, Vietnamese, Filipino, Korean, and Asian Indian), Hispanic (Mexican, Puerto Rican), African American, Native Americans, and Middle Easterners, in that order.

Of the thirty most ethnically diverse cities in the nation, twenty-nine of them are in California and one in Hawaii. But nothing beats San Francisco for that melting pot look—or "Chop Suey," as Rodgers and Hammerstein penned in their less than classic musical *Flower Drum Song.*

They Do Things Differently There

The city of Berkeley in 1989 passed a law exempting the miniature potbelly pig from its ordinance banning "livestock" within city limits. The pig is a pet to Vietnamese and others. Some voters opposed the exemption, worried that it might "impose domesticity" on a wild animal.

The *Sunday Chronicle and Examiner* proposed to include a free sample condom in the home-delivered Sunday paper but abandoned the idea after 53 percent of the readers polled objected. The other 47 percent wanted the condom, badly.

The North American Man-Boy Love Association (NAMBLA), a pedophile group that openly advocates legalizing sexual relations between men and young boys, held its monthly meetings at the Potrero Hill branch of the San Francisco Public Library for over two years until a reporter from KRON-TV infiltrated the group with a hidden camera in 1992, setting off a furor that resounded for weeks.

It turned out the library officials had no idea what the acronym NAMBLA stood for. Furthermore, the group's application to use the facilities was outdated. But in the ensuing "reformation" of library meeting qualifications, the directors did not prohibit NAMBLA from using the space. They simply decreed that NAMBLA would have to fill out a new application and that all meetings of any group would be subject to monitoring by officials. "The American Nazi party could probably meet in the main library since we have security there," an official said.

Renato Corazza, speaking for NAMBLA, said, "We don't want to be treated any differently from other groups," adding that the boy lovers would return to the halls of literature.

No doubt buffeted by high winds at Candlestick Park, Giants announcer Ron Fairly proclaimed, "Last night I neglected to mention something that bears repeating."

Undercover raiders from the California Department of Fish and Game descended on the Yau Hing pharmacy in Chinatown and found, among other illegal items, tiger penises, bear gall bladders, shark tails, antlers, rhino horns, and poached abalone. These animal parts are used in ancient Chinese medicine but strictly controlled in California. But it's just as tough to eliminate the trade as it is to control the flow of cocaine and opium, rangers say. Each bear gall bladder brings $400 to $600 in San Francisco and five times as much in Korea, to which they are smuggled.

After the 1989 Loma Prieta earthquake devastated the Bay Area and interrupted the third game of the World Series between the Giants and the A's, San Francisco instituted its own unique form of postquake assistance to the victims. It wasn't financial help with rebuilding their homes, although the federal government provided some of that, and much of it is still unspent in 1994. No, it was free, public "holistic massages" administered outdoors in the Marina District.

Interviewed on national TV about the quake, the ubiquitous columnist Herb Caen said of San Francisco, "Well, at least we figured out how to stop the Oakland A's."

While the '60s may be long gone, the fashions of that period have remained in San Francisco, even more so in the '90s than ever before. The corner of Haight and Ashbury now has a Ben and Jerry's ice cream parlor, decorated with a huge mural of cartoon cows. Small, boutique fashion shops offer polyester pants, bell-bottoms, mood rings, and posters of Charlie's Angels. "We're dealing with kids whose parents raised them with a kind of organic Hippie mentality," said the proprietor of a trendy clothing store called New Government.

When San Francisco became the first major American city to institute a domestic partner law (in 1989), vociferous critics from organized religion (particularly the Catholic church) warned that the City would be overrun by homosexuals with AIDS bankrupting the public treasury with their health care costs. That never happened, however. To the contrary, the City made money by charging thirty-five dollars to register the partners.

How soon they forget. While there is talk in 1994 of the Oakland A's leaving the Bay Area because they can't match the heroics of the (traditionally favored) San Francisco Giants, it's worth recalling that the A's stuck with Oakland through many long years of the Charlie Finley ownership era. The team still holds the record for the smallest attendance of any game in major league history—634 people on a cloudless night in 1978, when the Seattle Mariners were in town. People said that Finley actually counted the ticket takers and hot dog vendors in the 634 heads. One year, Finley didn't want to pay radio announcers, so the A's games were broadcast on a student station in Berkeley with a listening reach of only three miles. Disgruntled pitcher Goose Gossage, later traded to the Yankees, said "I know that winning isn't everything, but with Charlie Finley, winning isn't *any*thing."

During the enormously popular Gulf War in 1991, the Board of Supervisors of San Francisco issued a proclamation declaring the City a sanctuary for conscientious objectors and enlisted military who did not wish to participate in the violence. The national reaction to this sanctuary idea was volatile, to say the least. Newspaper editorials around the nation decried San Francisco as a traitorous city; some conventions canceled their bookings; merchants and the mayor pleaded with the Board to reconsider its motion. When voting a second time, however, the Board reiterated its offer of sanctuary to war resisters. As some kind of compromise, however, it also authorized a parade for the returning Gulf War veterans. Compared to the hysterical, patriotic fervor of such parades in other cities, San Francisco's version was subdued. The City That Knows How ain't gonna study war no more.

It happens every spring. The Bay to Breakers foot race attracts over a hundred thousand runners who traverse the seven miles from the Bay to the ocean side of the City dressed up in flipped-out costumes suitable for Halloween or *Beach Blanket Babylon*. The Bay to Breakers race is annually sponsored by the *Examiner*, and it's such a major event that the mightier *Chronicle* cannot ignore it altogether, so it has reported on the race without mentioning the *Examiner's* sponsorship. Petty, petty.

Nothing is more interesting to real San Franciscans than finding a choice parking space. The City has 464,000 registered cars but only

306,000 legal street parking spots. Some people pay the equivalent of the cost of a small condo to own a private parking garage space.

In Los Angeles, palm trees are considered a civic pride. But in San Francisco, after the 1989 earthquake reduced the Embarcadero Freeway to rubble and the Port Commission decided to put in palm trees in its place, the citizenry got up in arms. Palm trees, people screamed, are dangerous. Their leaves could fall off and kill someone. Rats would make nests in them. Finally, palm trees are just too . . . too *L.A.*, the protesters said.

The Larkin Street Youth Center as early as 1984 began offering help to adolescents who live on the streets of San Francisco, doing intravenous drugs and prostituting themselves for survival money. Only 25 percent of the homeless teens in the City actually come from the Bay Area; the others arrive from all parts of the country. Counselors from Larkin Street don't even try to convince the youths to go back to their parents; their emphasis is on clean needles and bleach for the intravenous drug users, condoms for the young male prostitutes.

The San Francisco Giants are the only team in major league baseball to offer health insurance and other spousal benefits to the same-sex partners of its employees. Candlestick Park is probably the only major league baseball stadium where you will routinely see gay couples holding hands or embracing each other in the stands. Not in the bleachers, though. It's a rough crowd out there.

Silicon Valley High

T hose funny guys down at Apple Computer in Silicon Valley, vicinity of San Jose, sometimes use the name of a famous person as a "code name" for a new computer they are developing. Charles Lindbergh and George Gershwin got their own computers that way, although by the time the machine is marketed, it is called something else.

Astronomer Carl Sagan was less than amused, however, to hear that Apple R&D had named a computer after him, and he had his lawyers write to Apple, demanding that they cease and desist what he called an unlawful use of his name for commercial purposes.

Fine. So what did Apple do? It changed the code name of the computer from "Carl Sagan" to "BHA," allegedly standing for "Butt-Head Astronomer."

Dr. Sagan then filed a full-bore libel suit against Apple, contending that the phrase "Butt-Head Astronomer" is defamatory and has subjected the famous scientist to "hatred, contempt, ridicule, and obloquy."

Now, the big question is whether the term "butt-head" is itself libelous or defamatory. Laid Back Enterprises in Oklahoma owns a trademark on a cartoon character named "Butthead," which it describes as "an endearing, fun-loving guy." Butt-head on MTV's "Beavis and Butt-head" cartoon show is something of a moron.

Perhaps the boys down at Apple don't have enough work to do?

The Foggy, Foggy Dew

Wayne Wheeler, founder of the Lighthouse Society in San Francisco, wasn't about to take it lying down when the Coast Guard abandoned its traditional foghorns in 1989 in favor of an electronic beeping device. The old-fashioned foghorns were simply too expensive to maintain, the government claimed. Wheeler considered the sound of the mournful foghorn as much a part of San Francisco's charm as the cable cars of the Golden Gate Bridge.

"You don't necessarily need these types of signals anymore, but I think you need the sound," Wheeler said. "You hear a foghorn, and you think of a forest of ship masts, cable cars going ding-dinga-ding, fog dripping off building eaves, and Sam Spade sidling down Hyde Street."

So he organized a whopper of a campaign to get the horns back and succeeded, at least for a few of them. City residents were quick to donate to the cause, and the owner of a shopping center offered to install a foghorn on his roof—aimed at Sausalito. But the first newly reinstalled foghorn was placed, where else, on Alcatraz Island. It was a dark and stormy night . . .

Soap Opera Titillates, Frustrates Bay Wags

Mayor Frank Jordan called it "a third-rate soap opera," but San Franciscans in 1993 were titillated by a City Hall love triangle gone wrong. Police department public relations director Joanne Welsh, who just happened to be the girlfriend of Supervisor Bill Maher, charged Police Chief Anthony Ribera with sexual harassment for allegedly fondling her—and giving her a pair of gold earrings. Ribera hotly denied the charges. Supervisor Maher then ordered Ribera not to dismiss or transfer Welsh from her job, improperly using his power to interfere in police department matters. He later apologized, saying he was going into therapy to work out his "clouded judgment." Then Maher and Welsh broke up, but she announced plans to take her harassment charges to the federal Equal Employment Opportunity Commission.

Got that? City residents did, but nobody knew quite what to make of it. Had Joanne really once been Anthony's girl and moved over to Bill, who then jealously attacked the chief? Ribera was the second police chief appointed by Frank Jordan to get into trouble; the first, Richard Hongisto, resigned after admitting that he had ordered his men to confiscate the press run of a gay newspaper that ridiculed his response to the riots following the L.A. Rodney King verdict.

"Life here feels like one big gossip column, and it's unfortunate," Richard DeLeon, author of a study on San Francisco politics, said. "We have some very serious needs in our neighborhoods, but we're not getting anywhere so long as this administration is preoccupied with embarrassing and degrading shenanigans."

In the midst of all the heat, Mayor Jordan sent his top political advisor, Clint Reilly, over to the *Examiner* office to complain about their coverage. Reilly got into a physical brawl with the executive editor, Phil Bronstein, and had to be driven off in an ambulance with sirens blazing, having suffered a broken ankle.

The *Examiner*, ever feisty, challenged Joanne Welsh to take a lie detector test. She accepted the challenge but flunked the test, twice. Then it came out that the polygraph test operator had been stripped of his license years earlier for incompetence. And *then* it came out that Supervisor Maher's counseling for this "clouded judgment" would be provided by his own sister-in-law, Dr. Mimi Silbert, who runs a San Francisco clinic for addicts and criminals seeking rehabilitation.

With a $184 million budget deficit and enormous problems of homelessness and crime, the City's bureaucracy came to a virtual standstill for weeks while the soap opera swirled. San Francisco is famous for its love of opera, of course, including the sudsy variety.

When You Think Wine, Think Gallo

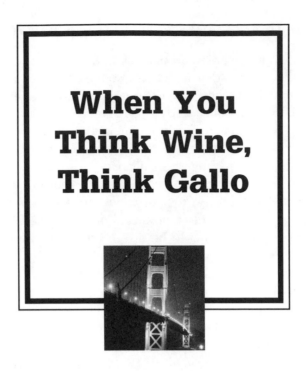

Joe Gallo Jr. was raised from age thirteen by his much older brothers, Ernest and Julio, after their parents died in a murder-suicide. Joe Gallo Sr., a poor Italian immigrant, was a ditch digger for the municipal sewer system in Oakland who worked his way up to owning 160 acres of vineyard in Modesto. He shot his wife, Susie, to death, then turned the gun on himself, in June 1933.

Sons Ernest and Julio expanded the family winery north of San Francisco, but their partnership never included their youngest brother, Joe Jr. So they were more than mildly surprised when he suddenly demanded a third of the Gallo empire in 1986, opening wounds in this family warfare that haven't healed since.

The bitter lawsuits between the brothers were waged over Joe Jr.'s decision to market cheese under the name Joseph Gallo Cheese. A simple enough name for his own product, you might say, but Ernest and Julio contended it infringed on the family business identity. Ernest called his brother's cheese "garbage."

Their wine company now makes one of every four bottles of wine sold in the United States and has annual sales of $900 million, thousands of acres of priceless northern California vineyard land, and a Greek-revival architectured mansion called Parthenon West. Known for its cheap jug wines, Gallo is now trying to upgrade to fine chardonnays and cabernet sauvignons.

With the mysterious deaths of the parents and the incessant, vicious squabbling between the brothers, the Gallo family seems to be saying that blood may be thicker than water, but wine is thicker than blood. So said Mike Gallo, Joe Jr.'s son, who himself is named after his great-uncle Mike (Joe Sr.'s brother), who was a kind of San Francisco Mafia don, with a criminal record for grand larceny. The elder Mike, it was said, paid off the cops and "fixed" judges in the Bay Area and its Wine Country for many years.

Despite any recent pretentions, the family fortune still has its roots in Thunderbird and other low-price, sweet, fortified jug wines favored by street drunks all over America because they're cheap and strong. Ask the guys in the San Francisco Tenderloin, and they'll tell you Gallo wine is as San Franciscan as sourdough bread and Rice-A-Roni. And pass the bag.

From Janis Joplin to Her Sister, Laura, San Francisco, 1966

Still working w/ Big Brother and the Holding Company & it's really fun! Four guys in the group—Sam, Peter, Dave, & James. We rehearse every afternoon in a garage that's part of a loft an artist friend of theirs owns & people constantly drop in and listen—everyone seems very taken w/ my singing although I am a little dated. This kind of music is different than I'm used to. Oh, I've collected more bizarre names of groups to send—(can you believe these?!) The Grateful Dead, The Love, Jefferson Airplane, Quicksilver Messenger Service, The Leaves, The Grass Roots.

Chet Helms heads a rock & roll corporation called the Family Dog—replete w/ emblem and answering service. Very fancy. Being my entrepreneur (and mostly having gotten me out here without money—I still have $30 in the bank I'm hoarding) Chet rented me this place for a month. He says if the band & I don't make it, to forget it & if we do, we'll have plenty of money. Chet is an old friend—married now to an actress named Lori. Tomorrow night at his dance, some people from Mercury will be there to hear the Grateful Dead (with a name like that,

Wild child Janis Joplin smiles for the camera, Golden Gate Park, 1968.
(*Bettmann*)

they have to be good . . .) and Big Brother et al. and I'm going to get to sing! Gosh I'm so excited! We've worked out about 5 or 6 numbers this week—one I really like called "Down on Me"—an old spiritual—revitalized and slightly bastardized w/ new treatment.

Janis was a vision of Kentucky straight bourbon, Hippie-Mama hair, and heroin of course, a mixture that brought her to an early death by overdose.

Let It Bleed

The Beatles had *Let It Be*, an album of love and light, and played their last public concert in Candlestick Park in San Francisco. The Rolling Stones had *Let It Bleed*, an album in "sympathy for the devil," and had a concert at Altamont Raceway in Livermore, in the East Bay Area near Oakland where the Hell's Angels stabbed a young man to death, beat and maimed other concertgoers, and indirectly contributed to three subsequent deaths.

The Stones themselves were never blamed for the violence and deaths, but Mick Jagger later said, "when I think about that kid getting murdered at Altamont, I think, it could have been me." What ever happened to sympathy for the victim?

In any case, Altamont revealed the dark side of rock and roll to a generation of flower children and effectively ended the Era of Love in the Bay Area. After Altamont, no psychedelic or rock gathering in San Francisco was considered safe. In fact, no public gathering is safe.

Not even an ordinary baseball game. The World Series of 1989 (an all–Bay Area affair between the San Francisco Giants and the Oakland A's) was interrupted by a killer earthquake. I once saw a fellow plunge

Hell on wheels: Hells Angels in 1982. (*Bettmann*)

to his bloody death in Candlestick Park; it was a few years earlier in the 1980s, when the Giants under manager Frank Robinson were a last-place dud squad, and a drunken San Francisco fan tumbled off the upper deck railing while screaming curses at the home team. Through the game, he had been yelling obscenities and downing jumbo beers. He was sitting just a few rows behind me, making such a scene that everyone except the beer vendors moved away from him. At game's end, he lurched for the guardrail and fell, fell, fell, crashing onto an elderly man seated below and wrecking a stadium chair.

A few years later, after a lot of public hand-wringing, the Giants abandoned the practice of selling beer in the stands. Now you have to stand on line at a concession stand and are limited to two jumbos at a time. One of these jumbos is enough, of course, to make an inexperienced beer drinker turn green, but the real Candlestick bleacher bums can down it in a half-inning's work.

Conspiracy
to Commit
Lunch

$\mathbf{F}$eeding the homeless may be a most charitable enterprise, prac-
ticed everywhere by Christians, do-gooders, and public relief agencies,
but in San Francisco by 1994, it had become a crusade. This is a city,
remember, that virtually invented homelessness as an American social
phenomenon. Never call a San Francisco bum a bum—he's a gentleman of the streets. And he's in plenty of good company, including
women and children. Nobody knows how many San Franciscans live
on the streets, only that there seem to be more every year. Some of
that is due to the U.S. economy, some to the traditionally liberal and
generous treatment the City has always extended to the less fortunate.

All that has changed under the new Matrix program, which requires
those receiving General Assistance to be fingerprinted, harasses the
homeless for sleeping outdoors even when the shelters are full, and
doles out harsh penalties for those who are late for 6 A.M. street-clean-
ing "work assignments," even if they have AIDS.

The day of the free lunch is not over, however. Under Matrix, the
police started arresting members of a group called Food Not Bombs,
which served food to the hungry in front of City Hall (in Civic Center

Plaza) every day for a year without complaints or problems until the new program began. At one roundup of these dangerous criminals, police confiscated two boxes of day-old bagels and a pot of cream of mushroom soup, with the reasoning that they could be contaminated.

The arrests failed to stop the ardent activists of Food Not Bombs, of course. Even the chair of the Board of Supervisors, Angela Alioto, condemned the Matrix program of cracking down on homeless and hungry folks. "It's like arresting Mother Teresa and her nuns for feeding the hungry on the streets of Calcutta," she said.

In the first three months of the campaign, more than fourteen hundred homeless people were arrested for "crimes" such as blocking the sidewalk, urinating, or "aggressive panhandling." Cops took away their shopping carts and dumped their life's belongings as trash. The city authorities claim the sweeping arrests are necessary to clean up San Francisco's homeless problem and eliminate its reputation as a magnet for homeless people; social workers and service advocates allege the crackdown is illegal and won't solve the problem. Jobs, therapy, and education are solutions; putting the homeless in jail alongside real criminals doesn't help anyone except retail merchants, who hate the sight of bums loitering around their premises. Those same merchants are the biggest supporters of Matrix.

Consider the cost, too, of appointing a city-paid lawyer to defend every homeless activist who's arrested (at forty-five dollars an hour). Food Not Bombs had 145 of its members arrested in a two-month period. "This is a real waste of time and money for the entire criminal justice system," said Assistant Public Defender Sean Connolly. "Who's being harmed when someone feeds the poor?"

Worse yet, the crack cocaine dealers in Civic Center Plaza are now having a field day. The police are too busy rounding up homeless people and food activists to spend much time on dopers. One fellow, mistaken by the dealer for a narc, was stabbed right on the steps of City Hall and left there bleeding copiously.

One small ray of hope comes from seventy-one-year-old Ruth Brinker, who has founded Fresh Start Farms, a project that will train the homeless to grow gourmet organic vegetables in vacant lots. Brinker also created Project Open Hand, which now serves three thousand hot meals a day to people with AIDS. The gourmet organic garden produce already has a market, too; Brinker has persuaded sixty restaurants to buy the vegetables when they're ripe and ready.

The only problem might come from desperately hungry people jumping the fenced gardens to steal the produce right out of the ground.

Up, Up, and Away

The story seems too funny to be true, but eyewitnesses say it really happened, and it even made the Herb Caen column. Peter Gaye, a San Francisco–based flight attendant for USAir, boarded a flight to L.A. on a free employee's ticket and settled himself comfortably not in his assigned seat but several rows back in the nearly empty plane. At the last minute before takeoff, another flight was canceled, and Gaye's plane filled up with paying customers.

A USAir official then boarded the plane and asked the man sitting in Gaye's assigned seat, "Are you Gaye?" The fellow gulped nervously and nodded yes. "Then you'll have to get off the plane," the official said. The real Gaye, hearing this, stood up and said, "Oh, you've got the wrong man! I'm Gaye." "Then *you'll* have to get off the plane," the official said.

At that point, a young fellow sitting in the middle seats jumped to his feet, waved his arms, and shouted, "Hell, I'm gay too! They can't kick us *all* off the plane!"

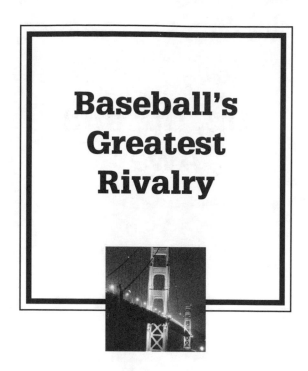

Baseball's Greatest Rivalry

Red Sox fans hate the Yankees, and Cubs fans hate the Cardinals, but these are at least civilized rivalries. San Francisco Giants fans hate the Los Angeles Dodgers with a fury and passion that has to be seen to be believed. It's more than rivalry, it's blood sport. Giants fans wish the Dodgers would all go down in a plane crash. "They seem to hate us," says Dodger manager Tommy Lasorda, "a lot more than we hate them."

It's true. When the Giants play in Dodger Stadium, they don't attract any more animosity from the home team rooters than other teams. Dodger fans, in fact, tend to be a bit blasé. They leave the game in the seventh inning, even if it's tied, just to beat the traffic on the freeway.

But let the Dodgers come to Candlestick Park and it's likely to provoke a riot, every time. The Giants will draw twice or more their normal crowd, and the game will invariably be marred by fistfights in the stands (God help a Dodger fan foolish enough to wear his L.A. cap or other paraphernalia), abusive language, objects hurled onto the field.

Armchair psychologists and newspaper pundits attribute this venomous outpouring of white-hot hatred to a deeper rivalry between the

A relatively peaceful day at Candlestick Park, 1993.
(*AP/Wide World Photos*)

two cities. San Francisco, once the grand empress of California, gradually lost her stature to the upstart growth in Los Angeles throughout the current century. Now, of course, L.A. dwarfs San Francisco in every category.

But as far as baseball goes, the Giants can beat the Dodgers, sometimes. When they win, all of San Francisco can gloat. When they lose, the misery is as thick as the morning fog over the Golden Gate. The rivalry is so intense that Giants fans consider their season successful even if they finish next to last, as long as the Dodgers finish worse.

As Time Goes By . . . Forty Years of Herb Caen in the *Chronicle*

"That Was San Francisco: The City was younger and gayer (weren't we all) and the four lines of streetcars rattled and crashed with a satisfying racket along Market St. You could ride from the Ferry Building to the Cliff House for a nickel, and you could ferry across the Bay for 21 cents. . . . You could walk down the street and nod hello to almost everybody, because you knew almost everybody. It was that kind of a town."
—DECEMBER 8, 1953

"These Things I Like: The weekend mobs on the Hyde St. cable, clinging happily to one another as they take the long slip-and-slide down Russian Hill toward the land of Irish Coffee. . . . The mournful clang of a ship's bell floating up from the Embarcadero in the post midnight hush, a seagull still as a statue on a Ferry Building piling, the rhododendrons bursting with prideful color behind the curlycued homes on Lombard St. . . . Grant Ave. in North Beach at night, with lights glowing dimly in shops filled with artsy-craftiness and distracted abstracts—and the sandaled shadows shuffling slowly past, boys looking like girls looking like men looking like crazy."

—MAY 12, 1957

"Nothing Ever Happens: The reporter looks out the window at the Old Mint across the street, its ledges lined with pigeons all in

a row. He stares at the old men sitting in the Mission St. sun, draped over their crutches, and wonders what they find to talk about. He cocks an ear to the sounds of the City: the siren sound of a fire engine threading its way down Market, a cop's whistle making the pigeons shift nervously, the sudden scream of a jet. A story in each sound, elusive and unattainable."

—DECEMBER 6, 1959

Herb Caen, *San Francisco Chronicle* columnist, 1977. (*AP/Wide World Photos*)

"A Kind of Anger: The City is becoming dangerously hardboiled, unsentimental and compartmentalized. The Ins and Outs have never been farther apart, and the Haves couldn't care less about the Have Nots, a sentiment that is returned in spades, redoubled. . . . Today, the only feeling that people at one end of Fillmore have for those at the other is to hope they don't come any closer. . . . Perhaps it is just as well that today's nostalgia is largely synthetic."

—APRIL 24, 1966

"The Walking Caen: Two teeny boppers walk by. They pause in front of Maison Mendesolle to light cigarettes, and I detect the cinnamon smell of marijuana. They giggle and walk on in a cloud

of pot. My my. Should I call a cop? . . . At the bottom of Powell, six young men with shaved heads and bare feet, with yellow robes between, are singing 'Hare Krishna' and ringing bells. . . . The tourists are going crazy, rushing into Woolworth's across the street to buy more film. . . . I guess it's a pretty colorful town, all right. And elegant too.''
—OCTOBER 13, 1968

"The Walking Caen: Scene: Hallidie Plaza, at the smelly foot of Powell at Market. Usual cast of characters: drummers, bummers, moochers, hootchy-kootchers, freaks, geeks, tourists taking pictures, pickpockets taking tourists, somebody's missing boy walking arm in arm with somebody's lost daughter. Dudes swagger among the prudes, offering everything from a sniff of coke to a stash of the old grasseroo, and trying to look anonymous among all this, the plainclothes cops in their fancy duds, inconspicuous as tarantulas on a wedding cake. . . . San Fransensual it is.''
—OCTOBER 24, 1974

"Drat the Drought: Mr. Sterling's 'cool grey city of love' has become the land of endless summer, but guilt keeps us from enjoying what the mindless radio and TV prophets still call 'another beautiful day.' Remember when as kids we used to chant, 'Rain, rain, go away, come again another day.' Remember rain, for that matter? . . . Remember galoshes, yellow slickers and old fashioned rain hats that looked like firemen's helmets? Gone, all gone, while we have baseball weather with no baseball.''
—FEBRUARY 20, 1977

"La Dolce Vita: Although I am not one of the noble 'born and raised,' I have lived here, man and boy, for 52-odd years, and I have never seen the City odder or more disturbing. Or perhaps disturbed is the word. At times the old line about San Francisco being the world's largest outpatient clinic seems to have come true. The nut quotient rises daily. . . . Violence simmers just below the surface of this city that dances on the edge of the world with gay abandon and abandoned gays. The killing fields are all around us, alive, sick, dying, and the band is playing louder and faster."

—SEPTEMBER 25, 1988

"And Then I Wrote: Know what I'm getting sick of? No, not prepositional endings. I'm getting sick of hypersensitive people. . . . An oversized women, waiting for a table at Fringale, asked the barman for a 'soft drink' and he handed her a diet Coke, which she took as such an affront that she wrote a seven paragraph letter of outrage. . . . Painful times at the S.F. Opera, which has both a big budget and a deficit. . . . Many a good head is rolling. . . . Also doomed at season's end: the opera shop on Grove. . . . Halloween sightem: a woman in a wheelchair who was wearing a striped prison uniform. Explained she with a smile, 'I thought it was a natural since they gave me the chair.' "

—NOVEMBER 3, 1993

Patty Hearst and High Anxiety

Heiress Patricia Hearst was only nineteen years old, living with her fiancé in a Berkeley apartment, when she was violently kidnapped by a gang of youths calling themselves the Symbionese Liberation Army (SLA). It was February 1974, a volatile time in the nation and the Bay Area. The daughter of Randolph Hearst, chairman of the Hearst Corporation, was snatched from the arms of boyfriend Steven Weed and held as a kind of political prisoner, ransom for the release of several SLA members held for murder.

The kidnappers demanded that the Hearst family prove their sincerity by giving away massive amounts of food to the poor. Hearst agreed, but the staged food giveaway turned into a wild riot, with people stampeding the food supply. From there, the nightmare grew worse. After seven weeks in captivity in a room the size of a closet, Patty seemed to be brainwashed. She announced in a tape recording that she had joined the SLA revolutionaries and taken the name Tania.

A few weeks after that, she was photographed holding a machine gun and assisting in a San Francisco bank robbery. After six of her colleagues, including her lover William "Cujo" Wolfe, were killed in

In the army now: In this first known photo of her since she was kidnapped, gun girl Patty Hearst models revolutionary gear while brandishing a semiautomatic, 1974. (*Bettmann*)

a shootout with the SWAT team, Patty and the remaining SLA members crisscrossed the nation on the lam. They surrendered back in San Francisco in September 1975.

The nation was transfixed by the ensuing trial, in which famed at-

Patty Hearst is brought to justice for holding up a bank, 1976.
(*Bettmann*)

torney F. Lee Bailey argued that Patty Hearst was victimized by the SLA and not mentally capable of understanding her crimes, but jurors gave her seven years anyway. She was pardoned by President Jimmy Carter after serving three and a half years and now lives in Westport,

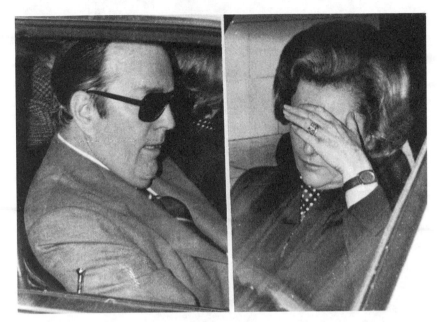

Randolph and Catherine Hearst en route to their daughter's trial, 1976.
(*Bettmann*)

Connecticut, with her husband, who was formerly her bodyguard, and two children.

Long removed from the limelight, Patty Hearst's story now seems just an antique anecdote from the heady years when young people (especially in San Francisco) rebelled against their parents and flouted the law. But her particular episode rocked the foundation of the City. It was horrifying enough when she was kidnapped, but when she joined the terrorist gang, it became high theater.

The Con and the *Chronicle* Editor

Dannie Martin and Peter Y. Sussman are an unlikely pair, but they were fated to meet. Martin, a.k.a. "Red Dog," is a lifelong small-time criminal who has spent most of the last thirty years in jail. Sussman is the editor of the *San Francisco Chronicle*'s "Sunday Punch" entertainment and commentary section. The convict from San Quentin wrote a compelling account of prison life and mailed it to the editor, who then published it. That's how it started.

Dannie Martin kept sending new pieces, some of them handwritten, to Peter Sussman, and his contributions to "Sunday Punch" became a regular feature. The authorities noticed and decided to enforce a law that prohibits felons in prison from publishing anything under their own names or getting paid for it. They also slammed Dannie Martin in solitary.

But he kept writing, now under the byline Red Dog, and Sussman kept publishing his extraordinary stories. They were filled with a kind of humor and good-natured acceptance of the author's unfortunate circumstances. They were wry, bittersweet, beautifully written tales.

Eventually, Martin was released, and in 1993 his book *Committing*

Convict and literary legend Dannie Martin a.k.a. Red Dog, placed in solitary confinement here following a particularly inflammatory article he penned for the *San Francisco Chronicle*, 1987. (*AP/Wide World Photos*)

Journalism (written with Sussman) was, also. The author got quite a lot of press attention, and not only in the *San Francisco Chronicle*. But the problem is he's back in jail on assault and battery charges and not able to appreciate the accolades. Martin got busted on a parole violation after getting into a car accident while drunk and high on heroin. "I'm a drug addict," he said. "There are no guarantees when you've been one as long as I have."

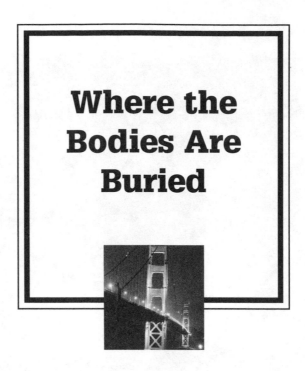

Where the Bodies Are Buried

In 1937, San Francisco was such a booming metropolis that it sanctioned the almost unbelievable practice of digging up the City's corpses—all of them—and shipping them ten miles south to a new burial ground in the village of Colma.

They didn't get all the bodies out, however. As recently as 1993, three hundred bodies, apparently of Gold Rush workers, were uncovered by accident while workers restored the grounds near the Palace of the Legion of Honor. An addition eleven thousand bodies may lie under the museum.

Meanwhile, Colma, with a population of only eleven hundred living people, is home today to a "population" of at least two million, maybe as many as three million, dead people. The whole town exists for its cemeteries, mausoleums, and crypts. It's a sleepy place, all right, a true bedroom community of San Francisco.

When the great job of moving the bodies was undertaken, the City became a macabre scene of rotting and ancient remains piled in the streets. Young men played soccer using old skulls for balls. Nobody ever made an accurate count of the bodies that wound up in Colma.

Where the Bodies Are Buried

Newspaper tycoon William Randolph Hearst, 1863–1951. (*Bettmann*)

Among the famous interred there, however, are the original William Randolph Hearst, who's in a crypt with a half-full bottle of Evian water, lawman Wyatt Earp, *Chronicle* founder Charles de Young, railroad barons and City aristocrats like Crocker and Spreckels, blue jeans pioneer Levi Strauss, slain mayor George Moscone, and Ishi, the last North American Indian.

And don't forget Emperor Norton, the dotty rice dealer who in 1854 proclaimed himself "Emperor of the United States and Protector of Mexico." He has a properly royal crypt. Thousands of household pets lie in peace here, too.

Colma itself, with no room for industrial development because of its fifteen spread-out cemeteries, has become a moderately exclusive, rich suburb. The city gives its residents free tickets to the opera and Giants games in San Francisco, all on the death taxes. It doesn't hurt that Colma features the Bay Area's busiest Kmart and shopping mall, either, or that the town just legalized gambling. Now you can place your bets in a field of lost souls, the builders of San Francisco under your feet.

Crime Blotter, 1962–95

As attacks on tourists at Fisherman's Wharf escalated, worrying the merchants who survive on the sales of T-shirts, boat trips to Alcatraz, and sourdough bread, crime in the present reflected crime in the past. Although they can't stem the tide of muggings, robberies, and random shootings of tourists in San Francisco, federal police announced they are reopening an investigation of the famous 1962 jailbreak from Alcatraz.

Former convict Thomas Kent confessed in 1993 that his fellow inmates Frank Lee Morris and brothers Charles and John Anglin escaped alive from the Rock and were probably picked up on shore by a girl-friend who drove them to Mexico.

The escapees converted a vacuum cleaner motor to a drill, Kent said. They crawled through their tunnel, slid down a pole, climbed a chain-link fence, and sailed off the island on a raft they had sewn together from raincoats smuggled into the prison. Authorities presumed them drowned at the time, but their bodies were never found.

The new evidence suggests that they may have survived, but it's hard to say how police can find them when they can't find the thugs who mugged and beat two Japanese women tourists near the cable car stop at the pier. Or the creep who attacked and robbed comedian Larry Miller outside the trendy Cannery comedy nightclub. Or the trigger-person who shot an Irish student in the back as she was finishing her dinner on Pier 39.

San Francisco used to call itself the City That Knows How. Now, it knows how to terrorize and maim, to instill as much fear as glamour, as much sadness as joy. The place has changed, and not for the better.

As long as the Bay glistens in the sunlight and fog rolls in over the Golden Gate, San Francisco will have charms, and good people will be drawn to its steamy, exuberant energy. But social trends of recent years have made it, like all American cities, less innocent and more dangerous. No Hippies are passing out free joints in Haight Ashbury in 1995. The cops won't even let homeless people alone to lounge in the parks. It's not an easy or laid-back lifestyle, but the City has the second most expensive overall cost of living in the United States, after Honolulu.

San Francisco exists in a dream, a mythical place of romance and intrigue. But in daily reality, it's a confidential memo on a battered desk at the downtown precinct, something some snake is up to, a tired parade of suspects in the same old street game of violence and squalor. There are blocks of the Tenderloin near downtown where it's dangerous by day and suicidal by night to walk around unprotected. It's a forkin' jungle out there.

It's a hard life for the street kids from the outer Mission or the underside of Oakland or the Asian ghettos. These young people see the great wealth of the City but have no chance for a piece of it except to steal and run. Anyone with anything is a target. It's a meat market.

If you remember how lovely it seemed, and you returned to San Francisco today after a long separation, you might be disappointed. You might not even recognize the town as the same place Tony Bennett crooned over. It's shabby at the edges. It's oozing with human catastrophes. Since the big earthquake of 1989, it's never regained solid ground.

But San Francisco will always be the promised land of the Gold Rush. In 1995, as California's Speaker of the House, Willie Brown, prepares to challenge Roberta Aschenberg and Frank Jordan for the mayor's seat, the value of that seat has multiplied many times over. San

Francisco inspires passionate concern in its citizens. It's too beautiful and too special ever to die, as long as people will literally risk their lives for the right to live there. Seismologists speak of a 90 percent chance of another devastating earthquake over 7.0 on the Richter scale, which could come today or tomorrow or twenty years from now. But true San Franciscans are unafraid of death. They already live on the edge. Nothing less than natural catastrophe will move them.

Index

INDEX

INDEX